Children as Story-tellers

Developing language skills in the classroom

Claire Jennings

OXFORD UNIVERSITY PRESS

For Paul, who tells such
wonderful stories

OXFORD UNIVERSITY PRESS AUSTRALIA

Oxford New York
Athens Auckland Bangkok Bombay
Calcutta Cape Town Dar es Salaam Delhi
Florence Hong Kong Istanbul Karachi
Kuala Lumpur Madras Madrid Melbourne
Mexico City Nairobi Paris Port Moresby
Taipei Tokyo Toronto
and associated companies in
Berlin Ibadan
OXFORD is a trade mark of Oxford University Press

© Claire Jennings 1991
First published 1991
Reprinted 1992, 1996

Copying for educational purposes
Where copies of part or the whole of the book are
made under Part VB of the Copyright Act, the law
requires that prescribed procedures be followed. For
information, contact the Copyright Agency Limited.

National Library of Australia
Cataloguing-in-Publication data:

Jennings, Claire.
    Children as story-tellers: developing language
    skills in the classroom.

    Bibliography.
    ISBN 0 19 553286 4.

    1. Story-telling — Study and teaching (Primary).
    2. Language arts (Primary.) I. Title.

372.642044

Designed by Steve Randles
Cover illustration by Rosanna Vecchio
Illustrated by Rolf Heimann and Melissa Webb
Typeset by Syarikat Seng Teik Sdn. Bhd., Malaysia
Printed in Hong Kong.
Published by Oxford University Press,
253 Normanby Road, South Melbourne, Australia

Contents

Introduction

This book is the outcome of many years of teaching children and thinking about how they learn language. It is the result of working with and observing children from a range of backgrounds and abilities.

Since the beginning of time story has been the vehicle for educating as well as entertaining. This textbook considers story-telling from both of these aspects.

Reflecting on the writing workshops with children in my classrooms and linking these with the story-telling process, I realised that I was not allowing children to participate in the total story experience. A successful story always has its origins in oracy. Most story-tellers, whether they be using the oral or the written form of language, begin to piece together their ideas with spoken words, talking out aloud to themselves, their friends, colleagues or family members, seeking feedback on the potential of their ideas as future stories. If children are to become confident with their literacy skills then we must allow them to share their ideas first. This can be done in a variety of meaningful ways. In the past this has often been restricted to the 'Show and Tell' timeslot. However, if children are observed in their play it will be noticed that they spend much of their time telling stories. They joke, yarn, tell riddles and recount past experiences. They are natural story-tellers. So why not bring this wealth of language into the classroom?

I have been working with many children across the primary school over the past two years. By constructing a story-telling workshop based on the framework of a writing workshop, I have seen children grow in confidence, both in themselves as people and as language-users. If children are confident orally, then it naturally follows that they will be more confident with their attempts at reading and writing. This strategy has been very successful with children who have English as their second language. By recounting personal experiences or retelling favourite stories, these children responded positively to this non-threatening activity.

Story is an essential feature of any culture. Without it we have no notion of who we are or how we fit into the scheme of life. And so in our classrooms we must keep story alive. We must read daily to our classes and build in time and space for them to tell, read and write their own stories. Children who have not been exposed to story are disadvantaged. They find it difficult to listen to and understand the points of view of others. Their experiences in life are often limited and so too are their powers of imagination. But we can help them. We can enrich and extend them through daily stories—those they hear in class and those we are willing to let them tell. We need not expect that they will always want to write them down. But we must encourage them to engage in this most enjoyable and non-threatening activity, and this book shows just how this can be done. Strategies for making children aware of different types of stories and story features are given, suggestions for making children's work public are provided, as is advice for the actual presentation, telling and performance of stories. The workshop based on the story 'Mother Snowbed' shows the practical implications of the story-telling approach for the classroom, and a guide for using story-telling across the curriculum is also given.

Children as Story-tellers is full of practical ideas to involve children in story-telling in ways that will be educational and entertaining, developing their language skills, and stimulating their interest in the spoken and written word.

Story-telling in the classroom: Why?

❝ *In every language, in every part of the world, story is the fundamental grammar of all thought and communication. By telling ourselves what happened, to whom, and why, we not only discover ourselves and the world, but we change and create ourselves and the world too.*[1] ❞

Aidan Chambers aptly sums up the importance of story in our lives. Through stories, whether they are retold accounts of our personal experiences or retellings of traditional or contemporary narrative, we are able to grasp a sense of language to make meaning, to structure our thoughts, to extend knowledge of ourselves and the world we live in.

Thus, story empowers us as learners. It is a familiar form of communication because we experience it from a very early age. Parents speak in narrative to their young, telling them stories about themselves, reading aloud from text, singing and chanting rhymes and fingerplays. Through these exchanges children internalise the features of narrative. They know about events and their sequence in a logical order, the notion of characters within the context of a story or yarn, and ideas about plot. What happened, to whom and why are questions to which children want answers.

Children are natural story-tellers

As children are continually exposed to this rich world of story, they internalise the structure of our language, reproducing phrases and sentences approximating what they hear. It is not surprising, then, that children become natural story-tellers, from the simple story of the two year old, 'Daddy, you a big bad wolfie', to the yarning based on the personal experiences of older children and the spontaneous story-telling that crops up outside classrooms released in casual conversations. Such verbal narratives have their origins in the form of story.

Children are still sharing, chanting and performing miniature stories, rhymes and jingles from long ago alongside of more contemporary compositions:

On top of spaghetti
All covered in cheese
I lost my poor meatball
When somebody sneezed.
It rolled off the table
And on to the floor
And then my poor meatball
Rolled out of the door.
It rolled in the garden
And under a bush
And then my poor meatball
Was nothing but mush.[2]

Miss Mary
Mack
Mack
Mack
all dressed in
black
black
black
with silver
buttons
buttons
buttons
all down her
back
back
back
she asked her
mother
mother
mother
for fifty
cents
cents
cents
to watch the
elephant
elephant
elephant
jump the
fence
fence
fence.

He jumped so
high
high
high
he reached the
sky
sky
sky
& didn't come
back
back
back
till the 4th of Ju-
ly
ly
ly.[3]

Regardless of origins or era, children everywhere reveal their creative bent for story-telling.

The universality of story

This predisposition towards telling stories is embedded in all cultures. Primitive peoples passed their leisure time by exchanging personal experiences, embellishing key events to entertain their audiences. Language most likely developed because of the need for communication. In the form of gestures and utterances, body language combined and developed into controlled units of sound, modified by thought processes.

Early story forms were attempts to explain the unexplainable and so there emerged myths and legends to explain problems such as how the world evolved and the origins of the human race. Explanations for emotions such as love, hatred and jealousy were shaped through folk and hero stories where good triumphed over evil and the wrongdoers were punished with eternal banishment to the underworld of Hades. The qualities of endurance and fearlessness were admired and so hero-figures possessed these traits. Early forms of the oral tradition were, then, reflections of people's self-perceptions.

Collections of folk-tales and myths and legends from all over the world revealed the universality of this sensitivity for story. Ideas and plots were duplicated across all cultures and it became obvious that all races, regardless of background and location, had amassed oral traditions similar in structure and content.

Oracy: The forgotten aspect of the curriculum

Having accepted the universality of story-telling with its origins in the oral form, and remembering the significance of this form in communicating ideas and emotions, we must realise the impact that oral language has on thinking and learning. By using spoken language in inquiry situations, children become actively engaged in learning. In regular classrooms, all too often children are expected to 'hang up' their playground conversations outside the door before entering the realms of silent endeavour. This dampens spontaneity and clouds thought processes, frequently leaving the learners confined to rigid textbooks and grade-level parameters.

One way of recognising oracy and its educational significance is through story-telling. From simple recounted stories at the infant level to the extensively embellished forms produced by upper primary and secondary students, story-telling assists the language development of the teller. As the reteller plays with the original story-line, drawing on comprehension abilities from the simplest form of recall to the higher levels of synthesis where new and creative avenues of thought shape the original version into a personal narrative, an awareness of the elements of story is revealed. The structure of story has the essential components of a beginning, middle and ending, and is often made more complex by the establishment of a problem which needs to be resolved. These elements are linked with internal rhythms which make the narrative flow in story fashion. Oral language lends itself to a richness of quality. The narrator has to paint word pictures for the listeners who then create some sort of meaning from the images. To convey meaning solely through language, the story-teller must carefully select words and phrases to communicate the intended emotions. A clear story-line must be created which has minimal characters who move the story along.

Preparation for written narrative

Once young language-users become confident with oral retellings they can transfer their stories into written format. This is where the surface structure of grammar can be checked and attended to. Children who can retell using their own words are in control of the discourse and can structure and punctuate at their discretion. In conferencing sessions with peers and teachers they can then edit if necessary. Chapter 8 looks at the links between literacy and oracy.

Advantages to students with English as a second language

For children who have English as a second language, story-telling in the classroom is a powerful medium for the use of language in a satisfying way within a meaningful context.

Story-telling workshops conducted in primary schools continually reveal the value of this strategy for developing language. Through the workshops, children with varying language abilities find a non-threatening medium in which to participate. There are no comparisons of an intellectual nature but only a desire to participate in individual or group story-telling sessions. All children respond positively to story, and so they listen eagerly to the narratives of their peers with a reverence that is inspiring. The story-telling sessions then become the medium for boosting the children's confidence.

Self-esteem

Story-telling becomes a favoured pastime when encouraged in classrooms, because of its non-threatening nature and also because of the potential that everyone has for it. There is little or no rivalry among the participants who are accepted for their personal anecdotes or challenging retellings. This lack of competition and fear enables all children to participate freely and provides an avenue for positive interaction with peers. The story experience outcome, then, has the effect of enhancing the self-esteem of those in the group. Observation of children in story-telling workshops has repeatedly shown that those with low self-esteem are the ones who benefit the most.

Case study: Sophia

The most spectacular example of this development of self-esteem was in the case of Sophia. Since beginning school Sophia had been withdrawn and had made no attempt to socialise with her peers. This led to her non-acceptance within class as she progressed through her schooling. Her speech was minimal, mostly in one-word or small-phrase utterances. Sophia was being withdrawn from the regular classroom for sessions with a specialist language teacher. At the end of a particular story-telling workshop Sophia was the first to volunteer in the story-sharing at the close of the session. She sat on the stool beside the burning candle, our symbol that a story-telling session was in progress, and began to tell her story. The session-taker was unaware of Sophia's background and immediately made notes to build in story-telling techniques to the group in future sessions. This was because Sophia was not making eye contact with her audience and had her head turned sideways, away from the children. Her voice was muffled and it was difficult to follow the story-line. However, after her story, the class applauded and Sophia returned to her spot beaming brilliantly.

After the session the workshop supervisor was informed by Sophia's teacher about the significance of this episode. Sophia had shown initiative for the first time and was reaching out for involvement with her peers. The specialist teacher had called to collect Sophia for her language session and had also witnessed this event. She now saw Sophia's potential for oral language and recognised the need to leave her in the class to develop both her language and social skills in an environment which would support and encourage her.

· ·

Summary

There are many other success stories like Sophia's. It is the aim of this book that teachers will see the relevance of story-telling in the classroom as a vehicle for developing not only spoken language, but also the self-esteem and social skills of all children.

CHAPTER 2

An educational focus

❝ *'Story' is a mystery that has the power to reach within each of us, to command emotion, to compel involvement, and to transport us into timelessness. 'Story' is a structural abstraction perhaps built into human memory, a way of thinking, a primary organiser of information and ideas, the soul of a culture, and the mythic and metamorphic consciousness of a people. It is a prehistoric and historic thread of human awareness, a way in which we can know, remember, and understand.*[1] ❞

Story-telling is an art form which not only crosses the boundaries of time and culture, but has always been a vehicle for conveying knowledge, feelings, thoughts and ideas. And so, there is a place for story-telling in the classroom.

Repeatedly, in situations where a teacher has wanted children to write, they become frustrated and the teacher becomes frustrated, all because some of them don't know where, or how, to begin a story. Their minds are not clear. They need to clarify their ideas before writing. They need to *talk* and *yarn* about past experiences, *retelling* and *innovating* their accounts.

As teachers, we know the personal and social implications of being competent in literacy skills and that reading and writing are central to the learning process.

For children to be competent in literacy, we need to build their oral language skills in preparation for reading and writing, and story-telling is one way we can do this. The oral aspect of literacy needs more attention in the classroom than it usually receives. And it should not just be slotted into the junior school only. Successful language programmes should continue to involve children in creating oral, as well as written, narratives throughout their school years. The skills are interdependent. Reading and writing need to be practised in order that oral skills are also developed.

Once children have had frequent oral encounters with the structure of story, they then have a better chance of transferring this structure to their writing and making successful predictions in their reading of narrative. Listed below are some of the reasons why we should include story-telling in the classroom. Story-telling:

- develops a sense of story
- develops thinking skills

- stimulates talk and spontaneous response
- helps people become more aware of their power as narrators and writers
- reduces inhibitions which stem from more traditional activities such as book reviews or formal discussions on character, setting and plot, etc.
- demonstrates the benefits of varied cultural backgrounds
- shapes ideas and experiences into meaningful units
- creates a story-telling culture in the classroom
- provides active participation in literature and language sessions.

Development of a sense of story

Through retelling known stories, children internalise the structure of story with the essential elements of a beginning, a middle and an ending. They become more aware of the characters, the setting and the plot. They realise the necessity of using language styles. Chapter 3 looks at the different types of stories for telling.

Development of thinking skills

Creating a personal narrative is a way of structuring past experiences. To add colour and purpose to the event, the story-teller dips into a wealth of ideas, clarifying thoughts and painting verbal pictures for the listener.

Simply recalling a story and telling it as closely as possible to the original version will leave the reteller struggling. The narration will sound disjointed and impersonal.

A successful retelling will always be one where the story-teller relies on recall for the plot outline but uses higher level thinking skills as they attempt to paint with flair an exciting narrative.

Prior to the final telling, the story-teller will have exhibited a number of skills; the teller will have:
- reflected on the content of the story to gain mastery
- integrated emotional responses in order to convey these to the audience
- analysed what aspects of the story to highlight and intensify
- used visual imagery to increase the potential for story recall and vocabulary
- judged the worthiness of a story for audience appeal

- outlined the sequence of events for easy recall
- devised a method of presentation suitable to the story and the intended audience
- formulated different ways of telling the story for a range of audiences
- assessed the effectiveness of the final version.

As children become committed to the task of story-telling they intuitively use such thinking skills. They have a responsibility to their story and their intended audiences, and they are keen to satisfy. The implementation of such skills occurs as a natural consequence of the activity.

The benefit to the writing of narrative is obvious, and children do transfer these behaviours to the process involved in their writing.

Stimulating talk and spontaneous response

Story-telling is primarily an oral activity. The sharing of a story with an audience gives the teller an opportunity to practise spoken language. Experience shows that the more opportunity we have for using oral language, the more expert we become.

Through this medium the speaker is able to develop and refine language skills. These include:

- stringing words and phrases together into meaningful units
- extending knowledge of vocabulary/increasing wordpower
- organising words, phrases, sentences and meaningful units into the larger context of a story.

When telling stories in groups, children exchange a variety of language before selecting the final version. This exchange is rich in meaningful talk, stimulating spontaneous verbal interaction.

Awareness of selves as narrators and writers

The confidence-boosting aspect of story-telling is invaluable. Children become empowered with the skills of listening, speaking, reading and writing. The four components of language are integrated in the one activity of story-telling.

It is this awareness of their ability to perform orally that is significant. Most people doubt their ability to captivate an audience. And yet we expect children to do it every time they write in the narrative genre. Too often we tell them that their stories go no-where, have no middle or have an unsatisfactory ending.

A polished oral narrative can so easily be transferred into an exciting, well-crafted and meaningful written narrative. However, we must always value story-telling in its own right: it is an end in itself with a rich and varied tradition.

Reducing inhibitions

A boring language programme relies too heavily on activities such as the book review or a set of comprehension questions. The less empowered language-users are restrained because their skills of critical awareness are not well developed, and those students whose language skills are well developed become bored with the predictability of the activities.

Story-telling is a refreshing way to overcome this. Through the meaningful discussions and preparations preceding the retelling, story-tellers overtly demonstrate their responses to the narrative. More importantly, they feel much freer to contribute because there is no threat of critical appraisal from the teacher. This uninhibited response allows children to interact in a more meaningful way with the content of the story.

Children responding to character descriptions or extending settings through the visual imagery technique (see chapter 4, pp. 32–6) are able to act upon the elements of story in a non-threatening way.

Benefits of varied cultural backgrounds

The ethnic diversity of classrooms is a reality for both present and future education. Successful educational programmes will always take advantage of this. The cultural mix creates a range of skills and ideas which teachers can infuse into groups across the class. This variety of cultural backgrounds helps to break down the language barriers which often occur in areas of high ethnic proportions, minimising fears and maximising hopes, aspirations and perceptions within a positive learning environment.

Shared input into story-telling activities from diverse cultural backgrounds will raise the level of achievement in a group. The range of past literature experiences that the children bring with them will provide a colourful mosaic for creating story.

Shaping ideas and experiences into meaningful units

Collective attempts at story-telling in classrooms are satisfying experiences for all participants. Teachers are able to monitor the stories which emerge from these sessions, checking at the early stages that meaningful accounts are being developed. As children become more talented they are able to shape their narratives with more expertise, taking care that their craft exhibits the elements necessary for a successful story to occur.

As children move from the novice stages to become more practised tellers, they will merge their ideas and experiences with traditional stories to create new blends. These accounts become valued pieces, both as oral and written narratives.

Creating a story-telling culture in the classroom

The cohesive atmosphere resulting from story-telling in the classroom is powerful. Although actual output stems mostly from individual or group work, when the class comes together to share the stories, a common alliance is created.

Class members inherit ideas, beliefs, values and knowledge by interacting and by sharing stories, and these are transmitted and reinforced over time. Individual expressions and tastes are respected and accepted by the group as a whole.

Instances have been observed within schools where other classes have regarded with awe the collective creativity and total unison of a story-telling classroom.

Providing active participation in literature and language sessions

Successful learning is active learning. Children are engaged in meaningful activities and situations where established goals are pursued. In the integrated classroom where literature is used to stimulate language, story-telling is the active agent for developing listening, speaking, reading and writing skills.

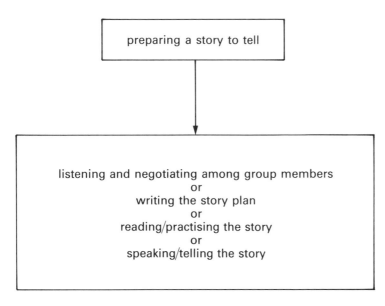

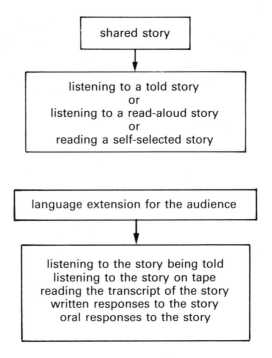

shared story

↓

listening to a told story
or
listening to a read-aloud story
or
reading a self-selected story

language extension for the audience

↓

listening to the story being told
listening to the story on tape
reading the transcript of the story
written responses to the story
oral responses to the story

Summary

The power of the oral tradition of story-telling, if used in the class-room, will strengthen the children's ability to structure their stories which can be presented to an audience both orally and in written form. A polished oral narrative can be transferred easily into an exciting, well-crafted, written narrative. Through this strategy, children are practising the skills of listening, speaking, reading and writing in an integrated language setting.

Types of stories to tell

❝ *In education there is increasing awareness that, if we want children to find reading, writing and learning as fascinating and exciting as some of us believe they can be, then we should ensure that they hear a wide range of stories. Language is central to most communication and the key to most learning.*[1] ❞

Children need to be exposed to a range of language genres in authentic contexts and to be able to experiment and use them for their own purposes. One of the key challenges for a teacher is to provide an environment that demonstrates and demands different uses of language. This chapter explores the use of oral language through story-telling.

Personal experience stories

Children have an instinctive feel for story, blending instances and episodes from their own experiences into oral narratives, therefore these personal anecdotes are natural items in a story-telling session. Exchanging personal experiences with peers is authentic because children identify with the similarity of events in other children's lives.

This focus on the folklore of children is what makes the work of poet-cum-storyteller Michael Rosen appealing to children. He talks about the notion of his poems as a means of arriving at literacy:

> All the nitty-gritty of everyday life for children has never been written about, but they can do it. They can do it, and they do. They do it with their everyday experience and with their own language.[2]

To initiate oral exchanges Rosen's poems can be used to stimulate children's ideas for creating personal experience stories.

Mini lesson

1 Tell Michael Rosen's poem 'Chocolate Cake'[3].

> I love chocolate cake.
> And when I was a boy
> I loved it even more.
>
> . . . Anyway,
> once we had this chocolate cake for tea
> and later I went to bed
> but while I was in bed
> I found myself waking up
> licking my lips
> and smiling.
> I woke up proper.
> "The chocolate cake".
> It was the first thing
> I thought of.
> I could almost see it
> So I thought,
> what if . . .

2 Have the children join in, using the action techniques listed below.

3 Divide the class into pairs to exchange personal experience stories. You can set the topic for beginning story-tellers. One of the children's favourites is 'spider stories'. Allow about five minutes.

4 Have the pairs regroup into fours. Children retell their spider anecdotes to the larger audience. Select a leader to choose the best yarn.

5 The selected representative from each group goes to the front of the class to recount their story to a wider audience.

Action techniques

Children are encouraged to polish their stories for public tellings by involving the audience. They can achieve this by building in:
- repetitive refrains
- finger clicking
- chanting in varying tones
- clapping
- echoing
- chiming-in
- whispering

and also by encouraging audience participation.

Group work, with the accompanying skill of co-operation, is not expected at first but becomes a favourite form of story-telling as children become more experienced.

Listed below are suggestions for spontaneous story-telling. Most children will have a personal experience story relating to:
- an embarrassing moment
- a dream I'll never forget
- spider stories
- food stories
- hobbies
- favourite films or TV shows
- our next door neighbour
- my worst best friend.

Below is a personal experience story by two grade 3 boys:

'Early one morning I got out of my bed
And went out of my bedroom.'

ECHO: **'Out of your bedroom ... Yeah!'**
CLASS: 'YEAH'

'I climbed up to the cupboard
and pulled out the lollies.'

ECHO: **'Pulled out the lollies ... Yeah!'**
CLASS: 'YEAH'

'Then I got down
and went into my bedroom.'

ECHO: **'Went into your bedroom ... Yeah!'**

CLASS: 'YEAH'

'I gave one to my brothers
And I ate the rest.'

ECHO: **'Ate the rest ... Yeah!'**

CLASS: 'YEAH'

'Mum found out and told Dad.'

ECHO: **'Told Dad ... Yeah!'**

CLASS: 'YEAH'

Dad said, 'Who's been eating the lollies?'

ECHO: **'Eating the lollies ... Yeah!'**

CLASS: 'YEAH'

'I said 'no', my brother said 'no',
and my other brother said 'no'.'

ECHO: **'We all said 'no' ... Yeah!'**

CLASS: 'YEAH'

'I said, 'My brothers are lying'
so they got a smack.'

ECHO: **'They got a smack ... Yeah!'**

CLASS: 'OUCII'

'AND I GOT AWAY WITH IT!'

Luke and Simon

Needless to say, the class's reaction was one of uproarious
laughter. It became a favourite story of the class and they were
invited to participate, hence the collective 'YEAH' throughout.

. . . .

Riddles

In traditional African story-telling there is a period of riddling
which precedes the actual story-telling session. This idea works
well with children because they all seem to possess a collection of
riddles, jokes and rhymes which they are enthusiastic to share with
others. Those children who have contributed to the riddling session
feel a sense of participation and the children who elect to remain
audience members are actively involved through the challenges of
guessing. A riddling introduction such as this sets the scene for the
story-teller to begin.

Retellings of original stories

Children are always eager to retell a story they have just read or heard and often want to work on the one told at the start of the session. They should be encouraged to select favourite stories from books they have read in the past. This can include any stories read to them by parents, teachers and librarians, or those they have experienced in their personal reading.

There are many advantages of allowing children to retell traditional or contemporary stories, including:

- children initially select old favourites which can be recalled immediately
- the familiarity which children feel with the known structure of previously shared stories enhances their confidence in their choices
- making a retold story their own by creating a personal interpretation based on their experience of the story.

Innovating known stories, poems and rhymes using vocal jazz

There are a range of ideas for bringing children and stories together. Once children are confident at exchanging personal experience stories, they can be challenged by a number of strategies for creating unique language patterns which can result in mini stories.

Combination stories

Take ideas and characters from various stories to create new stories. Titles can be listed in columns and details from the story can be added below, for example:

LITTLE RED RIDING HOOD	THE THREE BILLY GOATS GRUFF
grandmother	the biggest billy goat
woodcutter	the middle-sized billy goat
wolf	the little billy goat
woods	bridge
basket	troll
cakes	dinner
bed	grass
flowers	water
axe	hungry
eat	horns

THE THREE
LITTLE PIGS
smallest pig
middle-sized pig
biggest pig
wolf
straw
sticks
bricks
pot
boiling water
blow
huff and puff

The new story could be devised by combining ideas from the above lists:

Once upon a time there was a troll who lived in the woods next door to a wolf. They were always fighting. Little Red Riding Hood didn't like fighting so she was always trying to make them friends. Over the other side of the hill lived a mad woodcutter who lived in a house made of sticks. The wolf and the troll decided to invite their friends, the three billy goats Gruff, to have a holiday. One night they all decided to play a trick on the woodcutter. The wolf went over to his house and began to huff and puff. The woodcutter became frightened and called out for help. Little Red Riding Hood heard all the noise and came running with her basket full of cakes. When the animals saw all the food they decided to leave the woodcutter alone and have a feast instead. Everyone lived happily ever after.

Vocal jazz

This strategy brings out the music in words and the class or group are able to celebrate their composition of a selection of words on a theme.

Mini lesson: Cars

Steps	Stages	
1 Show children a selection of cars from magazines and advertisements	ALL:	Cars, Cars, Cars (*whisper*) (*finger click*) noises of cars made by the children
	ALL:	Cars, Cars, Cars (*louder*) (*finger click*)
2 Choose names of four cars	SOLO 1:	Holden
	SOLO 2:	Ford
	SOLO 3:	Toyota
	SOLO 4:	Volkswagen
3 Choose types of cars	ALL:	racing cars, diesels, taxis, tow-trucks, bright cars, dented cars, slow cars, bombs.

4	Choose four types of trucks	Repeat three times, gradually becoming louder.	
5	Choose noises cars make	ALL:	screech, skid, slide, roll, crawl, speed, jerk (*repeat twice*)
6	Choose parts of cars	SOLO 1:	steering wheel, seatbelt, engine
		SOLO 2:	roof-rack, radio, window
		SOLO 3:	boot, door, windscreen-wiper
		SOLO 4:	muffler, brakes
7	Repeat first verse		

Vocal jazz can take on other forms. On page 26 is a composition performed by a group of grade six children. It is related to a theme on 'weather'. The children were divided into three groups. Group 1 performed the jazz chant according to varying tones (indicated in parentheses). Group 2 echoed group 1. Group 3 chimed in with a related retort.

This strategy can also be used with nursery rhymes. By stringing together bits and pieces of known rhymes and jingles, children can create interesting stories prepared for performance by adding, chanting, chiming in, echoing, finger clicking, clapping or whispering features.

On page 27 is an example created in a story-telling workshop with a group of grade 3 and 4 children. A range of nursery rhyme books were given to the children. This group selected traditional rhymes with retorts in contemporary language. The chants were performed by three pairs and four solo parts.

Point-of-view stories

Traditional tales can be retold from the point of view of one of the characters. Using *Jack and the Beanstalk*, select four children to tell the story from the point of view of Jack, his mother, the giant and the cow. Divide the class into four groups and have each child tell their version to a group.

Weather

Name: _____

GROUP 1 chant   GROUP 2 echo   GROUP 3 chime-in

GROUP 1 (*softly*)   GROUP 3
GROUP 2 (*echo*)

Rain Rain
Rain Rain
Dark clouds
are here again

(*chanting louder*)
Swish Swosh
Snow Sludge
Oozing mud
Like chocolate fudge

(*chanting louder*)
Scream Breeze
Gale Storm
Tempest never
let it rest

(*Blast*)
T-U-R-B-U-L-E-N-C-E
(*swinging arms and bodies
spinning*)

(*whispering chant*)
Gale force winds
are gone again
Gentle breeze
Is here to stay

Pitter patter
on the roof

(*sing to known
tune*)
Rain drops keep
falling on my
head

(*chant and chime-in*)
Rain rain go
away,
Come another
washing day

(*monotone*)
On a dark and
stormy night
All the people got a fright

(*shout*)
S-U-N-S-H-I-N-E

ALL: (*sing to tune of known song.*) You are my sunshine
My only sunshine
You make me happy
When skies are grey
You'll never know dear
How much I love you
Please don't take my
Sunshine away.

Contemporary Nursery Rhymes

Name:_____

CHANT 1:   Jack and Jill went up the hill
CHANT 2:   But where is Little Miss Muffett?
CHANT 1:   Jill fell down and broke her crown
CHANT 2:   Miss Muffett is sitting on her tuffet.

ALL SING: Baa baa black sheep
           Have you any wool?
           Yes Sir, yes Sir
           Three bags full.

CHANT 1:   Up Jill got and home did trot
CHANT 2:   While Miss Muffett eats curds and whey
CHANT 1:   Jill's head will mend without a bend
CHANT 2:   But the spider frightened Miss Muffett away.

ALL SING: One for the master
           And one for the dame
           One for the little boy
           Who lives down the lane.

SOLO 1:   Oh where, oh where has Humpty Dumpty gone?
CHANT 3:   He's smashed up all over the floor, stupid.
SOLO 2:   But Little Bo Peep has lost her sheep.
CHANT 3:   That's none of your business sticky beak!
SOLO 3:   Little Boy Blue fell asleep on the job.
CHANT 3:   No pocket money for him this week then!
SOLO 4:   Oh where, oh where has my little dog gone?
CHANT 3:   You shouldn't have pets if you can't look after them.

R
PAGE

Newspaper stories

Ask the children to read as many newspapers as possible, select an article which interests them and create a story around it, for example:

Three Australians found adrift in Atlantic Ocean

UFO sightings over Ayers Rock

Skeletal remains discovered in cellar

Instant stories

Providing children with a variety of objects or aids helps to stimulate ideas for stories. These may consist of:

- individual bags holding a range of items such as a key, some finger puppets and an apple
- a series of pictures from magazines or newspapers
- a tape with voices and noises
- cards featuring characters, settings and a plot or situation
- a card with the ending of a story
- a card with the beginning of a story
- a song or poem
- a poster
- a range of objects on a tray.

Time is allowed to prepare a short story or yarn around these props. Instant stories can be used as ice-breakers at the beginning of a session and can be especially suited to the novice story-teller who has difficulty thinking up original ideas.

Instant stories will also reveal to the teacher how more experienced story-tellers are developing their skills of characterisation, setting and plot.

Magic box stories

Place an elaborately decorated box, which is empty, on a table. Children take turns to imagine its contents and construct a story around them. Children must be aware of communicating clearly what the object is used for, how big it is and who would use it.

Imaginary journeys

Encourage the children to relax in a comfortable position, and ask them to close their eyes as a narrator takes them through an imaginary journey. The narrator must be careful to establish a clear sense of setting and of characters, describing both in detail for the listeners to create visual images. More advanced narrators can weave in a plot.

> You are walking along a sandy beach. The tide is lapping against your feet. In the distance you can see the outline of a tall, stooped figure walking towards you . . .

Mime stories

Children can mime stories as they are being told by an adult story-teller, a child story-teller or a taped story. The enactments provide an interesting backdrop to the story.

Summary

By using a range of styles to stimulate story-telling, teachers can motivate all children regardless of their background knowledge of the story process. Ideas presented in this chapter will help bring words, which are the tools of stories, alive. Children who enjoy some of these activities will move on to become lively, independent story-tellers.

Strategies to develop awareness of story features

Story is still at the heart of our classroom teaching, but we are anxious that the children be the storyers, that they develop their story sense, and come to not only experience story but partake in it, working with its inner worlds and outer forms to create ever-increasing circles of meaning.[1]

To understand the power behind story, children need to master the elements of story. They need to be familiar with the characters, setting and plot. They also need to develop their mastery of words so that they can convey their stories in a captivating manner.

If we can help them to realise the puzzles and powers of the characters, not just as they appear on the surface, but also their essence, their inner thoughts and how their actions determine the outcome of the story, then we are equipping children to conquer the world of narrative.

As teachers we must give children strategies to explore the elements of character and setting and to develop exciting story-lines. They can then use this knowledge to structure their own stories more effectively.

As children meet the challenges of character, setting and plot in stories and manipulate them to produce innovative variations, they are metastorying, going beyond the initial version, reflecting and responding entirely through their own experiences with, and prior knowledge about, stories. This is how children create their imaginative variations.

Story-telling then becomes a forceful meaning-making medium where teachers can encourage reflective responses via a number of strategies. These will be considered below.

Visual imagery

If used in the context of story-telling, visual imagery helps children recall episodes from the story and the details necessary to embellish the plot.

Setting

Visual imagery is successful in developing vocabulary to describe settings in a story. For a story to be successful, the listeners need to gain a sense of setting.

After telling a story, have the children close their eyes and take their minds back to a setting in the story. Tell them that their minds are like a camera lens, and they must zoom in for a close-up look. Allow a minute or so for them to create a visual representation in their minds. Ask them to concentrate on the physical surroundings and any moods conveyed through their description. They are then able to produce a range of elaborated descriptions which help them later in recalling the story for telling and which also assist their retelling with a range of appropriate words to use. Then ask individual children to relate their descriptions to the class.

During a telling of *The Tinder Box*[2], the teacher can demonstrate the use of visual imagery, by modelling his or her imagination as the story is being told (or read):

A soldier came marching along the road: 'Left, right! Left right!' He had his knapsack on his back and a sword by his side, for he had been to the wars, . . .

> . . . All right, children, I see a distant horizon. Along the dusty, isolated road, coming towards me, there is a stooped figure. It seems to be the figure of a man but it is hidden in the shadows of the ghostly trees hanging over the roadside. Lonely boulders huddle near the edge.

Encourage the children to concentrate on the setting being described. Allow them to make their own additions while first introducing the activity. A sharing of these images helps children grasp the idea of visual imagery instantly.

Character

The same process can be used for developing a sharper sense of character. After telling *The Tinder Box*, have the class close their eyes and take them back to a character in the story. As they zoom in for a closer look, draw their attention to the external features of the character, encouraging a wide range of responses. After a telling of *The Tinder Box* begin:

OK, children, I have a clear picture of the soldier. He is stooped over with exhaustion from his long period fighting in the wars. His clothes are as dusty as the road and his empty knapsack hangs limply by his side. His sword looks like he does, no longer shining, but dull and defeated. So disillusioned is the soldier that he does not look up . . .

On the road he met an old witch—a horrid-looking creature.

Children, this witch is so stooped that her nose is nearly touching the ground and her eyes are slits of darkness. Her cape is torn and tattered and she looks slyly backwards towards the approaching soldier.

Initially, children will select ordinary words such as 'good', 'nice', 'lovely', 'dark', etc., but as they become more experienced, and if they are continually immersed in a range of literature, then their descriptions become more vivid. They will choose words such as 'old crone', 'gloomy', etc., which are more powerful and convey deeper layers of meaning, helping to create atmosphere for listeners.

They begin to infer meaning from these exterior features and so include personality traits; a much higher level of thinking is occurring at this stage. For example, after describing the witch in the above story, they might assume from her narrowed eyes and sly body language that she was up to mischief and not to be trusted.

It is important to develop characters beyond judgements based on appearances only. Children will learn to make inferences about character traits from the visual images they receive from story.

As children openly relate their character descriptions they are always fascinated by the similarities and/or differences which occur in the various accounts. It is important to point this out as a valid occurrence; there is no right or wrong response to a story, only varying shades of meaning.

Visual Imagery in Story-telling

Name: _____

1 When you are telling _your_ stories
  Do you think about your _characters_?
  ● What do they look like?
  ● How do they dress?
  ● How do they make you feel?
  ● How do they behave?
  Do you think about the _setting_?
  ● Can you describe different parts of the setting?
  ● What are some of the details which help to paint a vivid picture
    in your mind?

2 If we can create a vivid picture of the characters and the setting in
  our minds, then we can remember the story much more easily. It
  also helps us to choose interesting words to use.
  **Pretend your mind is a _camera_, and _zoom in_ to get a close-up look
  at the main characters.**
  ● What do you see?
  If the character is a witch, you might see a wrinkled face with skin
  as thick as leather; gnarled fingers wriggling on the end of bent
  arms; a hooked nose which casts a bleak shadow across these
  fearsome features.

R
PAGE

A written record of the descriptions on a wall chart or the chalk-board can be incorporated into a class, small group or individual retelling or can be referred to if the children are transferring their oral narratives into written form. Such lists can also be integrated into spelling programmes.

Character model

Another activity that helps to develop a sense of character is to use a dummy (dress-maker's model) and dress-ups (this activity can be presented in stage 3 of the workshop; see chapter 6, pp. 61–2). Select a group of children to dress the dummy. They can take up to fifteen minutes or so because the language arising from this activity reflects the range of ideas that emerge from the interactions of the group members. By negotiating, the children agree on a common character. They have created a visual image which has grown out of their oral exchanges.

The group then returns to other activities while a fresh group comes to the model. Their task is to develop a narrative inspired by the character of the model.

When they have completed their story, the participants sit or stand around the model and tell their story to the class. Some groups will complete a narrative in one session. Others may need more time to develop their plot.

The main purpose of this activity is that children become aware of the importance of character when devising a story, because character-types determine the outcome of the plot.

THE TINDER BOX

Character Study

Witch	Soldier		'Friends'
	Before	After	
creepy	dusty	gay	gay
selfish	bold	fun-loving	fun-loving
crabby	adventurous	romantic	selfish
cruel	selfish	lonely	untrustworthy
scary	untidy	happy	creepy
nasty	greedy	rich	scary
grumpy	tired		
unkind	sad		
mean	poor		

Setting Study

The road	Inside the tree	The city
dusty	dark	large
long	musty	colourful
bumpy	candle-lit	tall buildings
tree-lined	wooden doors	horses
	dirt walls	crowded
	dogs	garden
		castle

R

PAGE

Story webs

Another strategy to aid children's understanding of a character is to create a story web. These can vary depending on the concept taken. For example, if you had just read or heard the story of Cinderella you might decide to do two types of webs: an emotional web and a character web.

Emotional web

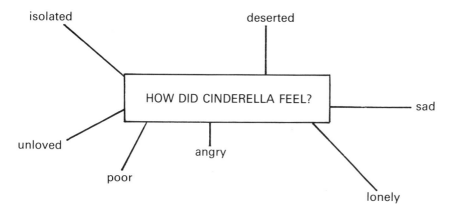

Character web

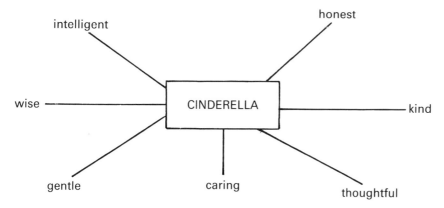

Word webbing

If we use a story the children are familiar with then we can list some story words. Children can build a parallel list of words which are related to the story but are not actually mentioned ('thinking words'). Once again children are encouraged to think beyond the surface of the story and relate the concept words to selected words from the story. This strategy is demonstrated using Hans Christian Andersen's story, *The Tinder Box*, where some of the links between the story words and the thinking words are indicated:

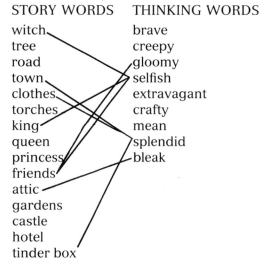

STORY WORDS   THINKING WORDS

This is a most effective strategy for creating visual imagery related to a story and, more importantly, for extending children's thinking beyond the story. If children can make meanings of their own, their imaginations will be stimulated, and they will be enthralled by the powerful world of story. They will create semantic webs like this one, a network of interrelated ideas and meanings:

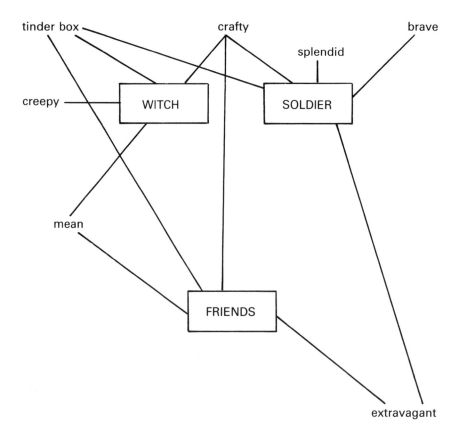

Story maps

Setting

Plotting maps of the development of sequences in a story will draw children's attention to the setting. This is an excellent strategy to employ along with visual imagery.

After children have drawn their representation of a story, you can have them 'zoom in' to particular positions on the map and paint the topography with words. If children are working in groups then the child who has the role of recorder could write down key words which describe the setting. A tape-recording of this activity will also provide material for the story-teller at a later stage if descriptions are needed to build into the story for retelling or to weave into a written narrative.

Plot

Story maps are useful strategies for recalling the chronological sequences of events for retelling. The visual representation of a map is easier to recall and children's minds are not overcrowded with too many details to learn. Below are two contemporary stories mapped in different ways to accommodate their varying structures.

Where The Wild Things Are by Maurice Sendak

A **circular map** is appropriate for this story[3] because Max goes on a journey and ends up back home, where he started.

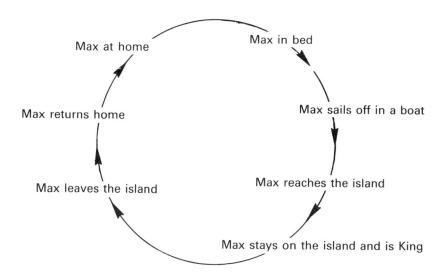

The Talking Bow Tie by Morris Lurie

This story[4] is a succession of events which lead on from the previous one, so the best structure is a **linear map**.

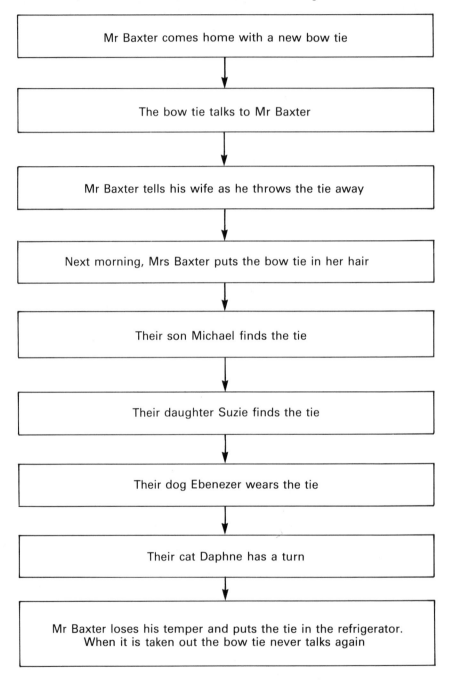

A successful retelling will essentially be the story-teller's personal interpretation which brings characters and setting alive using appropriate language, but which usually adheres to the author's original intentions.

Stories within stories

Often a story will be complex and will contain miniature stories within the framework of the main story. Innovative story-tellers will be able to isolate these instances and build them into new creations. Children who are alert and sensitive to the nature of story will infer new meanings and through inquiry processes, will take the story beyond the original meaning intended by the author. When these behaviours occur, it becomes obvious that the story-tellers are truly independent.

Summary

By these strategies, children's understanding of themes, events and characters are clarified and story experiences are extended. It is not necessary to perform 'surgery' on every story used with children because this would undoubtedly destroy many illusions for them. However, strategies such as those described above do equip children with tools for experimenting with the elements of story and give them greater power over oral and written samples of their own.

Techniques for story-telling

❝ *A fairy tale, like a cat, has nine lives, it can pass into many queer shapes and yet not die.*[1] ❞

To become a competent story-teller, it is necessary to realise the importance of technique. It is HOW a story is told that captures an audience. The teller must make an impact on the audience and each story will be presented in different ways, unique to that particular story.

If children are to become successful story-tellers, we must make them aware that the power of the story being told lies in the presentation. A good story told well will have more than nine lives, living on in the memories of the teller and the listeners, but told poorly, it will fade into insignificance.

Selection

The golden rule for selecting which story to tell is that the teller should LOVE the chosen story. This will ensure an enthusiastic delivery which will enthral the listener. The beginning story-teller should select a favourite and known story, for example, *The Three Billy Goats Gruff*. This can be accompanied by nursery rhymes which can be embellished using ideas suggested in chapter 3. Immediately, you have an instant story-telling session with minimal preparation necessary.

Folk- and fairy-tales have strong story-lines with interesting characters and lots of action. There are many collections available which children can read.

Children have a natural sense of humour and they love to play with traditional tales. The Reader's Theatre scripts in chapter 8 (pp. 78–83) reveal this talent. Michael Rosen's quirky collection, *Hairy Tales And Nursery Crimes*,[2] stimulates children to rework traditional tales, creating titles such as 'The Silly Ghosts Gruff'[3] and 'Handsel and Gristle'.[4]

Many children will commence their story-telling experience with personal anecdotes. This is ideal. Simply provide them with techniques for presentation to make them aware of their audience.

Preparation

The idea of learning a story to tell deters many adults, and children can be just as vulnerable. Suggestions for preparation will assist them in commencing. The guide on p.44 can be enlarged and displayed in the classroom or it can be handed out for personal use.

Evaluation

A sense of audience is important for story-telling. Use the checklist with children to perfect their presentations.

Story aids

Once children know HOW to tell stories successfully, they may wish to use aids to accompany the telling. Younger audiences, especially, respond to visual stimuli, including any of the following items.

Puppets

There are many types of puppets which children can use to assist their story-telling. They can be made to accompany personal experience stories as well as traditional tales such as *The Little Red Hen*[5] and *Little Red Riding Hood*,[6] and contemporary tales such as *Where the Wild Things Are*.[7] If no more than five or six puppets are used, then all children have equal opportunities to participate in the preparation and the performance. Types of puppets that can be used include:

- favourites from home
- sock puppets
- paperbag puppets
- papier mâché puppets
- covered plastic bottles with sticks inserted into the neck for easy manipulation
- paper plates
- finger puppets.

Guide for Learning a Story

Name: _____

1 Read the story silently.
2 Reread the story out loud. You may wish to read it on to a tape or to a friend.
3 Draw a map of the story, inserting the main events.
4 Make story cards for each event. Number them and keep them in sequence. This gives you the outline of the story.
5 Memorise each card in the correct order.
6 Reread the story a few times or listen to the tape. Good times for listening to tapes are when you are in bed before you go to sleep or while you are getting dressed in the morning. Use your 'Walkman' if you have one.
7 Memorise the first few sentences (the introduction), and the last few (the conclusion).
8 Memorise important speeches from each character.
9 Now try retelling the story in your own words, but keeping close to the original story-line.
10 Have you decided to use any aids?

Presentation Checklist

The story

Name: _____

- Do you know the story-line?
- Will your beginning captivate the audience?
- Was your conclusion satisfying for the listeners?
- Did you need to memorise any important sentences or phrases?
- Are you confident to use your own words for the rest of the story?

The language

- Are you aware of word power?
- Think of the words in your story which you can bring alive.
- Did you make your characters LAUGH, DANCE, SING, WITHER AWAY or WOBBLE?
- Choose ten words in your story into which you think you can breathe more life.
- Practise saying them in more interesting ways, then go back to the story.

Your body

- Do your EYES help tell the story? When your words SING, or SIGH, make your eyes do the same (your audience will be entranced).
- Do you need to change your facial expression for any of the characters?
- Are you communicating with your audience? Lean slightly forward to establish contact. Use your arms, etc., for gestures, but don't overdo it. If you need to move about, make sure the audience can see your face if you are speaking.
- Can your audience hear you? If it is necessary to whisper or speak in low tones, keep it audible or you will lose your listeners.
- Remember the power of the PAUSE. If you pause in a key position you will have your audience waiting expectantly.

R
PAGE

Sand

Sand can be used as a medium for story-telling in a number of ways including:
- gathering around a sand pit while the story-teller draws symbols from the story during the telling
- making a transparent sand tray and placing it on an overhead projector; characters and symbols from the story can be drawn as the story is being told and the images will be projected onto the screen.

String

String can be used to create shapes consistent with ideas and characters in a story. Children enjoy experimenting with a piece of string or wool which has been tied into one piece and is manipulated by the hands and fingers. Two excellent references for this activity are *Cat's Cradle And Other String Games*[8] and *The Story Vine*.[9]

Story-boards

A regular story-board will be approximately 60 cm × 45 cm in size and so there is a limit to the number of shapes that you can stick onto it at a time. Larger story-boards made of cork or polystyrene are satisfactory if they need to be transported.

Story-boards can be used in a number of ways:
- cover a flat board with felt and use felt cut-outs from the story. Place each piece on the board as the story unfolds (this is an excellent memory aid for beginning story-tellers)
- use paper or material cut-outs strengthened with iron-on stiffening or Velcro. These surfaces will stick to a felt board or you can use Blu-tack to stick them around the room, or onto children or up the wall as you tell the story
- using a long strip of paper, draw the story in frames and unfold the paper as each section develops.

Overhead projector

These are often locked away in dusty cupboards in the library. They can be reinstated in the classroom and children love the effects created with them:
- sand stories (see above)
- place coloured cellophane cut-outs from the story onto the projector and you will see enlarged coloured images on the wall or screen
- shadow shapes can be cut out and placed onto the projector and these will give dark images.

Slides

Take photographs of the illustrations from your favourite story and develop them as slides; project them onto a backdrop as you tell your story. Alternatively, you could photograph children dramatising a story, and develop them as slides for added atmosphere.

Odds and ends

Collect interesting trinkets, statues, labels, signs, hats, coats, masks, tins, candles, torches, musical instruments, sound tracks, etc., to aid your story-telling. Some story-tellers add items of clothing as they tell the story or poem. In a telling of 'The Ballad of the Drover' by Henry-Lawson[10] you can add items of a stockman's clothes as the story unfolds. These could include cabbage hat, vest, old shirt, baggy pants, boots and a whip.

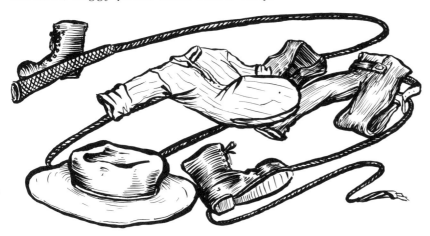

Chalk stories

- Draw a map of the story in the school yard using chalk; take the audience through the story, drawing in the characters and adding in details to the setting along the way (use the map for your cues).
- Embellish a story with chalk-board illustrations during the telling.

Story skirt or apron

- Sew large colourful pockets around a skirt or apron and place items used in your stories into each pocket. Children will be delighted as you retrieve items as you relate the yarn.
- Allow children to draw from the pockets and tell the related story.

Story basket

Allow children to choose an item or set of items from a basket placed nearby. Tell the story associated with the selection.

Bards and minstrels

Have the children bring their stories alive by:
- dancing the tales
- singing poetry and stories
- group recitals and performances.

Paper stories

Fold or tear paper into characters and images from the story. Children will be delighted as accordion figures and other images appear while a story is being told. Two suitable references for paper stories are *Down Amongst the Gum Trees*[11] and *Paper Stories.*[12]

· ·

Creating atmosphere

These suggestions to aid story-telling help children create an atmosphere of wonder and awe which will inspire their listeners. This can be extended by darkening the room for spooky stories. In a telling of *The Ghost-Eye Tree*,[13] the curtains could be closed, the lights turned out, and the story could be told as illustrations from the book were projected onto the wall using an overhead projector. When this technique was used, grade 1 children huddled together in this haunting setting and the tale became a favourite request in their weekly library sessions, with the darkened atmosphere being the drawcard. Other ideas for creating atmosphere include:

- sitting outside under a canopy of trees to tell a story set in a forest

- using classroom furniture to create suggestive settings, for example an instant castle will emerge by rearranging and stacking tables and chairs
- spotlights can be used to highlight the narrator and other participants during the telling; the atmosphere can be changed by placing coloured cellophane over the light.

Audience participation

Many stories lend themselves to audience involvement. Children can be encouraged to chant or sing refrains and choruses which recur throughout a story. They can be helped along with signs displayed on the blackboard or on pieces of cardboard. In a telling of *The Little Red Hen* the children made large signs which were held up to encourage the audience to call out the refrains, 'Not I', said the cat, 'Not I', said the dog, 'Not I', said the mouse.

Story packages

Teachers may wish to build up packages for classroom use. A package could include:

- a copy of the story for the children to read
- a breakdown of the story on small cards numbered sequentially
- hints for telling the story
- suggestions for presentation.

For example, a package on *The Talking Bow Tie* by Morris Lurie could include the items on pages 50–1, in addition to the copy of the book.

Story package   Name: _____

Mr Baxter comes home with a new bow tie. He decides to wear it out to dinner that evening. He showers, dresses, and puts on the bow tie.

↓

The talking bow tie says to Mr Baxter: 'You look ridiculous'. → Mr Baxter tells his wife about the bow tie as he throws it away.

↓

Mrs Baxter puts it in her hair. The bow tie says to her: 'Your nose is too long. Your eyes are too small. They look like raisins. In fact, your face is one of the silliest faces I've ever seen'.

↓

MICHAEL
'Don't be ridiculous ... Your head's like a rubbish tin with the lid jammed on crooked ...' → SUZIE
'Oh how gorgeous!' 'But you're not' said the bow tie.

EBENEZER
'What a smelly dog. He smells like over-cooked cabbage. He smells like ...' → DAPHNE
'You look like mouldy cheese. You look like a cross-eyed mop.'

↓

Mr Baxter put the bow tie in the freezer next to the fish fingers and left it there for three days and three nights.

↓

And when he took it out, believe you me, that talking bow tie never spoke again.

Hints to the children for telling *The Talking Bow Tie*:

- use a different voice for the bow tie and try to keep it the same all through the story
- remember to change your facial expressions to suit the mood of the characters
- keep looking at your audience
- your voice must be strong and clear
- if you are using aids, make sure they add to the interest of the story: don't let them slow you down or take your eyes away from the audience for long.

Suggestions for presentation:

- find a bow tie or make one out of material or paper. You can pretend to be each character as you tell the story and put the bow tie on then throw it away each time
- have papier mâché puppets or stuffed toys in front of you. They can represent the characters and you can place a bow tie on each one as the story unfolds
- use a felt board. Place felt cut-outs of the characters on the board when appropriate
- draw each scene in chalk on a large board as you tell the story.

Summary

The most important thing to remember with story-telling is that it must be FUN for the story-teller and for the audience. If children know some basic techniques which will enhance their presentation, then their confidence will soar and they will have a successful session. Variety in presentation creates an atmosphere of excited expectation. If this standard is repeated for each performance then a keen story-telling atmosphere will develop within the classroom (and maybe even throughout the school).

The story-telling workshop

❝ *. . .there is no greater gift a writing teacher can give than to help another person know he or she has a story to tell.*[1] **❞**

A successful teacher who is concerned with oracy and literacy will know that all children, regardless of background, possess stories to tell. In the past, failure to recognise this fact has resulted in too many children being deterred from speaking and writing for an audience because they have had teacher-selected topics imposed on them. Research has shown that children must be allowed to choose their own topics for writing if we want them to feel positive and confident about the task.

In a story-telling workshop children work on anecdotes, yarns or retellings which they select, practise and polish for a public performance. The following story-telling workshop is based on the tale *Mother Snowbed*, by the brothers Grimm.[2]

The workshop consists of four stages:

- *Stage one*: Orientation
- *Stage two*: Teaching point
- *Stage three*: Workshop
- *Stage four*: Sharing and performing.

Stage one: Orientation

The whole class gathers at a central point to listen to a shared story being told. This is where the workshop begins, and children's later attempts at story-telling benefit from this demonstration.

In this initial stage of the workshop, a competent story-teller (guest story-teller, teacher, librarian, parent, etc.) begins the session with a story.

To engage the children in the process, a candle is lit which signifies that story-telling is in progress. This, or other rituals, may be performed whenever story-telling occurs and children learn to associate the symbol with rapt attention. A special rug or mat spread out on the floor can also be the signal to sit and listen to or share stories. Some groups like the presence of a chair as an invitation to sit and tell. A rocking chair or large cane chair will do.

OTHER NOWBED

A widow had two daughters, one of them beautiful and hardworking, the other ugly and lazy. But she much preferred the ugly and lazy one, because she was her real daughter, and the other one had to do all the work and be the kitchen drudge of the family. She forced the poor girl to sit down every day at a well by the roadside and spin till her fingers bled. Now it happened one day that the bobbin got quite covered with blood, so she stooped down with it over the well and tried to wash it, but it slipped out of her hand and fell to the bottom. She cried, ran back to her stepmother and told her about the mishap. Her stepmother gave her a terrible scolding and was so hard-hearted as to say: 'Since you let the bobbin fall down the well, you can jump in yourself and fetch it up again.' The girl went back to the well and had no idea what to do, and in her terror she jumped in to fetch the bobbin. She lost consciousness, and when she woke up and came to herself again she was in a beautiful sunlit meadow covered with thousands and thousands of flowers. She walked on through this meadow and came to an oven full of bread; and the bread was calling out to her: 'Oh, pull me out, pull me out, or I'll burn—I'm baked to a turn already.' So she went up to it and took the bread shovel and lifted all the loaves out one after another. Then she walked on and came to a tree, and it was covered with apples and called out to her: 'Oh, shake me, shake me—we apples are all ripe and ready.' So she shook the tree, and the apples fell down like rain, and she shook it until there was not one left on the branches; and when she had put them all together in a pile, she walked on again. Finally she came to a little house with an old woman looking out of it; but she had such big teeth that the girl was scared and turned to run away. But the old woman called after her: 'Why are you afraid, my dear child? Stay with me, and if you do all the housework nicely it shall go well with you. You must just be careful to make my bed properly and give it a good shake to make the feathers fly, because that's when it snows in the world; I am Mother Snowbed.' Hearing the old woman speak to her so kindly, the girl plucked up courage, consented to serve her and set to work. And she did indeed look after everything to the old woman's satisfaction and always gave her bed a mighty great shake, making the feathers fly around like snowflakes. In return she was very well cared for, never given a harsh word and fed every day on roasts and stews. When she had been with Mother Snowbed for quite a time she began to feel sad, and at first even she herself didn't know what the matter was; finally she realized that it was homesickness. Although she was ever so many times better off here than she was at home, nevertheless she felt a longing to go back. Finally she said to the old woman: 'I've got sick for home, and although it's ever so nice down here I can't

stay any longer, I must go back up to my family.' Mother Snowbed said: 'You are a good girl to want to go home again, and because you have served me so faithfully I will take you back myself.' Then she took her by the hand and led her to a huge gate. The gate was opened, and just as the girl was standing under it a great shower of gold poured down, and all the gold stuck to her so that she was completely covered with it. 'This shall be yours, because you have worked so hard,' said Mother Snowbed, and she also gave her back the bobbin that she had dropped into the well. Then the gate was closed, and the girl found herself up in the world, not far from her mother's house. And when she entered the courtyard, the cock was roosting on the well there, and he sang:

> 'Cock-a-doodle-do, doodle-do,
> Our golden lady is back, doodle-do.'

Then she went into the house, and seeing her arrive all covered with gold her mother and sister gave her quite a welcome.

The girl told them all that had happened to her, and when her mother heard how she had got so rich she wanted to see the same good fortune come to her other daughter, the ugly and lazy one. So she told her to sit by the well and spin; and so that there would be blood on her bobbin, she pricked herself in the finger and stuck her hand into the thorn hedge. Then she threw the bobbin into the well and jumped in after it. She landed, like her sister, on the beautiful meadow and walked along the same path. When she got to the oven, the bread again called out: 'Oh, pull me out, pull me out, or I'll burn—I'm baked to a turn already.' But the lazy girl replied: 'And get myself all dirty? I should think not!' And she walked on. Soon she came to the apple tree and it called out: 'Oh, shake me, shake me—we apples are all ripe and ready.' But she answered: 'The very idea! One of you might fall on my head,' and with that she walked on. When she came to Mother Snowbed's house she wasn't scared, because she'd been told about her big teeth already, and she

entered service with her right away. On the first day
she forced herself to work hard, obeying Mother
Snowbed and doing everything she told her, thinking
of all the gold she would be given. But on the second
day she had already begun skimping her work, and on
the third she grew idler still, even refusing to get up in
the morning. Also she didn't make the snowbed
properly or shake it to make the feathers fly. Mother
Snowbed soon got tired of this and dismissed her from
her service. That was well to the sloven's liking, for
now, she thought, the shower of gold will fall; and
sure enough, Mother Snowbed took her to the gate,
but as she was standing under it a great cauldron full
of pitch was poured over her instead of the gold.
'That's your wages,' said Mother Snowbed, and shut
the gate. So the idle sister got home, but she was
covered all over with pitch, and when the cock that
perched on the well saw her, he sang:

'Cock-a-doodle-do, doodle-do,
Our dirty black slut is back, boo-hoo.'

And the pitch stuck fast to her, so that she was never
able to rub it off for the rest of her life.

Stage two: Teaching point

Some aspect of story is demonstrated through a variety of techniques and responses. The aim of this stage is to develop a sense of story and a knowledge of the elements of story. Strategies from chapter 4 are used here.

Visual imagery

Character

Mother Snowbed
- Pretend your mind is a camera lens. Take a close up look at the widow. What does she look like? Describe her facial features, her posture, her clothing, her reactions. Repeat for her daughter, her step-daughter, and Mother Snowbed.

Setting

- Close your eyes and zoom in on the path in the garden below the well. What do you see?
- You are inside Mother Snowbed's house. Describe what you see.

Story map

To develop an awareness of plot and story structure, map the main events in the story.

Story webs

Character web

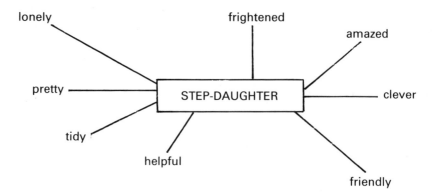

Appearance web

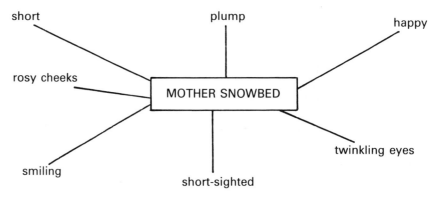

This is an important stage in the workshop because it is here that the teacher encourages the children to focus on the different elements of story. If we expect them to speak and write in the narrative genre, then we must equip them with the necessary tools.

Before children attempt to learn or create a story, they need to be able to recognise specific structures.

Types of story structure

Children already bring to the workshop an intuitive knowledge of the structure of story. They know about orientation, that is, that a story begins somehow, somewhere and that a complication develops. For the story to be successful these problem(s) must be resolved. We can draw the children's attention to this structure directly by making them aware of the different types of story.

Being aware of the types of story structure helps the story-teller to reconstruct the plot. Quick recognition of plot structure leaves the teller more mental space for adding details to embellish the story.

The basic narrative structure therefore consists of:

- *orientation*: the characters and setting are established
- *complication*: a problem or problems arise, which may be a series of related events
- *resolution*: the problem or problems are resolved satisfactorily.

Within this basic structure there are variations or patterns. Storytellers need to recognise these patterns which become the key to memorising the story outline.

The most common story types, and the most popular with young children, are the cumulative and circular stories. The repetitions and natural rhythms of cumulative stories provide predictable structures for children when reading or retelling. Active readers and listeners like the rewards of successful estimations of the action and outcome in the story-line. Linear stories are easy to recall as they present a series of events that occur in chronological order.

Stories which encourage audience participation through refrains, chants and repeated choruses are also most successful. These features can be built into most story types when adapting them for telling.

In a classroom where storying is a continuing activity, children become acquainted with a range of story forms. The familiarity with different forms aids their reconstruction of known stories and assists them in creating their own.

· ·

Stage three: Workshop

Children work individually, in pairs or in small groups, practising and creating their stories.

The working classroom takes on new dimensions as busy groups of children set themselves up in various corners of the classroom, or nearby rooms, with each group focusing on a particular stage of their rehearsal. Groups may be:

- creating a new story
- rehearsing their story
- writing drafts
- working on character-stories around the model
- making aids to assist the story-telling
- listening-post activities.

Oracy skills at work

Group story-telling

Every aspect of the preparation for group story-telling involves TALK. This begins with selecting a story to tell:

- all group members must agree on the chosen story
- all members must feel that their contributions and ideas are worthwhile
- all members must realise that the final version will be a melding of composite ideas
- for the telling to be successful, all group members must participate.

The skills of negotiation and co-operation are practised continually. Children are learning how to construct exciting narrative through talk. Usually, one member chooses to write down the transcript of the story as it emerges. This safeguards against omitting chunks vital to the plot or words which intensify meaning.

At this stage, groups are demonstrating the prewriting and first drafting stages of the writing process.

There are many benefits of group creativity:

- the interaction of the children improves the quality of the retelling
- children's imaginations are stimulated by this interaction and they often innovate or make changes in the original story, recrafting it to suit their personalities and the situation
- group retellings often involve theatre and all children respond to entertainment
- group retellings have audience appeal as classmates like to see the performance potential of their peers
- children identify with their age group and so respond positively
- this positive response encourages others to have a go at story-telling, and so peer modelling is a feature.

Individual story-telling

Children practising stories for solo performances are also engaging with language. As they practise their story, they are using oral language; if they are using a published story, they select ideas from the original and embellish them with their own words. The confidence they gain from the process as well as the actual telling help them become more proficient language-users. Workshop participants become totally committed to their task. This is because:

- the atmosphere is positive
- all contributions are valued
- each child has a meaningful role
- the task has a purpose.

Stage four: Sharing and performing

In the final stage of the workshop, the class regroups to share samples of stories from those children who have prepared their stories to a performance standard. Below is a retold version of a contemporary story called *Tom's Trousers*[3] by a grade 4 boy, which was presented at the sharing time in the workshop.

One day there was a boy called Shannan and he got a pair of pants for Christmas. They were a bit too big for him so he asked his mother if she would take an inch off them. The mother was too busy knitting and she said no. He asked his father but he was too busy fixing the car. Then he asked Grandma. Grandma was too busy watching TV. And then he asked Grandpa and he was too busy as well. So poor Shannan went to bed and while he was asleep his mum thought 'poor Shannan' so she took an inch off the pants. Then Dad thought 'poor Shannan' so he took an inch off the pants. Everyone took an inch off the pants. Then when Shannan woke up next morning his pants were like shorts.

'And I'm wearing them now.'

Shane

This stage can last for approximately ten to fifteen minutes. The success of this stage depends on the feedback received by the children when performing their story. Audience response is generally very supportive and the performance aspect gives the children a purpose for the workshops.

Summary

The structure of the story-telling workshop gives children a familiar framework within which to operate. They feel secure in the knowledge that each session will be structured similarly. The first and final stages, where they meet as a group for sharing, provide authentic purposes for the workshop. The sense of achievement when telling their story to the group is closely linked to the entertainment value of the process. Regardless of ability or background, all children respond positively to the celebration of story through story-telling.

Beyond the story-telling workshop

Our narrating serves different purposes. Sometimes we narrate in order to inform someone of something; sometimes to persuade someone to change a course of action; sometimes for pure enjoyment. Whatever the ultimate purpose this use of language is serving, we certainly use this function far more than we think we do.[1]

Once a story-telling culture emerges in the classroom, there are numerous possibilities for projecting beyond the workshops. Setting up situations for wider audiences helps bring story ALIVE. This chapter looks at a range of ideas for extending story and story-telling.

Festivals

With their atmosphere of entertainment and amusement, festivals are ideal opportunities for children to participate in set themes. Different festivals can be used in different ways to involve children as story-tellers.

Bookweek

This is an ideal annual opportunity to advertise a story-telling event. Children see the purpose of their stories going public and become enthusiastic about the performance aspect. They can be responsible for promoting the festival, making up captions and posters to attract interest.

Library ALIVE STORY-TELLING Festival

21st July

Time: 1 to 2·30 P.m

Bring your FAVOURITE book

Grades 5+6 will entertain you with stories gALORE

Come to the cosy corner by the canteen every recess this week for stories that will keep you awake at night, make your hair stand on end, and force your toenails to curl. From a group of Gr. 6 dudes

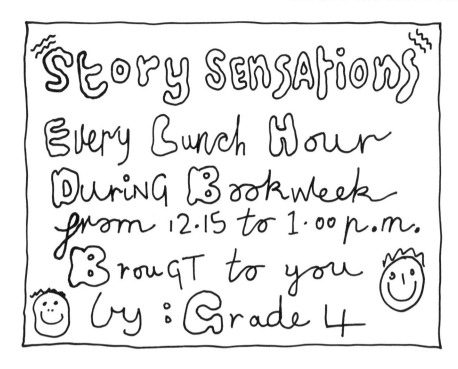

Town criers and broadsheets can also be used throughout the school as media for promoting the week's festivities.

School fêtes

Story Hours can be successful features of school fêtes. Children will be guaranteed enthusiastic audiences and may charge small admittance fees to raise money for the school. Added attractions may include:

A special tent could be set up for the occasion, creating a wonderful carnival atmosphere.

Folk-tale festival

This can be a way of concluding a unit on traditional literature where children present to the school, either in smaller sessions or at whole school assemblies, stories and plays related to the theme of traditional literature. Each class could be responsible for contributing to the festival, for example dramatising stories, dressing up as favourite folk-tale characters, parading their own designs of picture-books, etc. Parental attendance could be encouraged, and the assembly/festival could culminate in a school community barbecue.

The physical education teacher could be encouraged to involve the whole school in a series of folk-dancing sessions which could also be performed in groups at the assembly.

Theatre

Dramatic narration

Story-telling is theatre when it brings the narrative alive for the audience. Using aids and the power of narrative, children become theatrical in their presentations and their words breathe life into the story. Movement can be introduced to aid the story-telling and creates an added dimension for the audience.

Dramatic performance

Professional theatre groups can be used to work with children when presenting stories publicly. For instance, during a bookweek festival on folk-tales, the local community theatre group became involved with a class of grade 4 and 5 children to produce a local folk- or fairy-tale. The approach taken was to allow the plot and developmental sequences to come from the children. They were stimulated by the theatre group through a series of workshops which focused on communicating through movement with the emphasis on group participation. No props were used. The children used body movements to symbolise images in the story. Throughout the period the children were urged to think of ideas for the story-line that they could relate to local features and identities, including local:

- buildings
- landscapes and seascapes
- historical events, for example shipwrecks
- character types, for example fishermen.

The children produced a riveting piece of theatre which they performed before the school and parents. The video-taped version was often borrowed from the school library for family and class viewing.

Publishing stories

There are many media for making public the stories which children write or tell. These include:

- picture story books
- class anthologies
- big books
- video-tapes
- audio-tapes
- school radio stations

- public readings or recitals for local radio stations, newspapers, libraries, retirement villages, hospitals, local agricultural shows, crèches, etc.

The wider community involvement gives children the experience of relating to larger groups of people outside their familiar circles. It helps to build their confidence and prepares them for some of the more demanding public speaking activities of upper primary and secondary school such as debates and oral research. Most importantly, it is a preparation for participating successfully in a variety of settings.

We see numerous occasions where children's choirs are taken outside the school to entertain. Think of the advantage for both audience and story-tellers when they take their stories to perform to sick children in hospital and adults in retirement villages. Most old people harbour a treasure trove of stories and would probably like to share some of these with children. Regular sessions could be established where these groups could exchange stories and yarns.

Picture story books, class anthologies and big books

To extend story-telling from the oral to the written form, children may decide on a picture-book format or they may choose to group class stories into anthologies. These have been popular for some time and can be included for class and school library appreciation. The Big Book format is also popular, particularly for larger audiences and shared group reading. Children who are still gaining confidence with public presentations can use the Big Books as an aid to presenting publicly.

Radio stations

Children who are initially threatened by an audience may perform their stories with greater ease over school radio stations which could programme times for story-telling and reading. In some smaller communities, local stations have children's sessions which may invite school children to share stories and poems with the public.

Video-tapes

This is an excellent medium for allowing children to preview their performance critically and to make adjustments for future tellings. It is also an ideal way of transporting children's stories to long distance audiences. An exchange programme between schools could be established where each school forwards a video containing a selection of stories for viewing. Feedback can be either written or a live video response. Phone link-ups can also provide instant responses in such situations.

Audio-tapes

This option is much cheaper than video-tapes and children can be responsible for the operation of taping their stories onto cassette. The organisation of audio-taping is not as demanding as that which requires video equipment because children are able to perform their stories in their spare time.

. . . .

Summary

There are endless possibilities for presenting stories to real audiences. The initial stages in developing a story-telling culture will be nurtured within the classroom, but once children realise the power of their performance they will be anxious to take their stories far beyond the classroom workshop. We must be creative in our ideas for making children's work public, by going beyond the classroom walls and involving the children in their own stories.

Literacy connections

❝ *Written language development draws on competence in oral language, since both written and oral language share underlying structures and since, for most learners, oral language competence reaches a high level earlier. As children become literate, the two systems become interactive, and children use each to support the other when they need to.*[1] ❞

This statement reminds us how intricately the four modes of language are linked. To be competent literally, we must first be competent orally. To extend our capabilities in literacy we need to work constantly on oracy skills.

Story-telling is an obvious strategy. The modes of listening and speaking have been discussed in previous chapters where much emphasis has been placed on the oral aspect of story-telling. Story-telling extends literacy skills because children are integrating the four modes of language. If children are constantly immersed in story through their personal reading, through listening to shared stories, as well as by the wealth of stories which pervade life, then their notion of story develops naturally.

With a true sense of story becoming firmly fixed in their heads, our role as teachers, then, is to help children to express more clearly their ideas and feelings about the world around them. To do this we need to empower them with the words that will express and extend their ideas about the stories they read and hear.

Fortunately, the publishing field of children's literature has become so extensive that there is a wealth of literature in which to immerse children. By encouraging children to read a range of literature by various authors we are supplying them with the tools for both oral and written narrative. The linguistic spillover[2] from shared stories and independent reading equips children with ideas about how our language is structured in order to make sense to an audience, and also how this language appears in print with various signals to give added indications of meaning for the reader.

When we allow children to write stories which are influenced by those they hear or read we increase the range of ideas on which they can draw to create their own stories.

These personal interpretations will vary within the class or group as children impose their experiences and ideas to create individual stories based on the original. Each story may have a different format. We must inform children that they have decisions to make when setting out their written stories. Layout will depend on features which include:

- dialogue
- paragraphing
- repetitive refrains
- choruses
- shape poetry or stories
- diary format
- journals
- chapter books
- picture-books
- comic strips.

Immersion in a variety of styles will allow the children to see their options for presentation. The ideas discussed in the rest of this chapter require children to be familiar with various formats for presenting written story.

Personal experience stories

The example of a personal experience story by Luke and Simon in chapter 3 relies on dialogue and echoing. The written presentation looks like this:

'Early one morning I got out of my bed.
And went out of my bedroom.'

'Out of your bedroom . . . Yeah!' (echo)

'YEAH.' (class)

'I climbed up to the cupboard.
And pulled out the lollies.'

'Pulled out the lollies . . . Yeah!' (echo)

'YEAH.' (class)

Luke and Simon

Their written piece included use of quotation marks to denote speech and was presented in couplets to assist reading the piece for chanting purposes. To enhance the written form the echoes were highlighted in bold print and capitals were used for the sections meant for whole class participation. The completed piece had a professional appearance which was achieved by emulating published material.

Traditional narratives

A group of grade 5 girls retold *The Talking Bow Tie* by Morris Lurie,[3] and wrote in traditional narrative style. They used dialogue signals and introduced natural pauses in the text by creating paragraphs. Their story begins:

One evening Mr Baxter came home with a mysterious package. It was small and wrapped in brown paper. He immediately opened the bag and said to his wife, 'I've bought a new bow tie, I think I'll wear it out tonight.'

'What a nice tie it is,' said Mrs Baxter. 'I think it will look very smart with your suit.'

So Mr Baxter went and had a shower. Then he put on his socks, underwear, a clean, white shirt and his trousers. He was about to tie the bow tie around his neck when he heard someone talking. 'I beg your pardon?' said Mr Baxter.

'That bow tie doesn't make you look smart. It makes you look ridiculous,' said the bow tie. 'In fact you are the most ridiculous-looking person I have ever seen.'

'Mary,' yelled out Mr Baxter as he flung the bow tie across the bedroom and ran to the kitchen . . .

Gemma, Carly and Laura

This format resembles text in most novels and other fiction which children read. The girls referred to the original text for ideas in setting out their own story.

When we give children authentic purposes for writing their stories we also give them authentic situations to practise the skills of proof-reading and editing. Below is the first part of an innovation on Michael Rosen's poem 'Chocolate Cake' written by a group of grade 6 girls.

Chocolate Cake

click " " " " We love chocolate cake click, yeah!

When our ^twin cousins were ~~small~~ young girls they loved chocolate cake. Sometimes they would have it for sweets after dinner & if there was any left they would have it for play lunch. the next day.
They would wait + wait for the recess bell to ring.
They would look at there watches, + bite there nails. ~~finally~~ (RING RING RING.) They rushed to there ^their ~~to lockers~~ bags got out ~~there~~ their chocolate cake. Went to the furthest ~~courner~~ corner of the school, made sure no won was looking ~~pealed~~ peeled back the ~~chocolate cake~~ foil and there it was......... the ~~choca~~ chocolate. cake. The thick crackly chocolate icing, light fluffy cream, ~~delicou~~ ~~delicuo~~ delicious and sticky rasberry jam and ^the light soft sponge. Next weekend it was ~~Becky~~ Tiffany's and ~~Olivia~~ Melissa's birthday ...

At this stage of their writing the girls were interested in getting the story onto paper. Editing features such as paragraphing and spelling checks were considered at a later stage. After a conference they decided to tell it in the third person, having one person as narrator for most of the story. All group members participated in the introduction and concluding chorus where they chanted their lines accompanied by finger clicking. Because they chose third-person narrative, their format resembled that of a story with paragraphs to introduce breaks into the text. Their final draft was completed on the computer and looked like this:

click! click! ... 'WE LOVE CHOCOLATE CAKE' ... click! click! click!

When our twin cousins were young girls they LOVED chocolate cake. Sometimes they would have it for sweets after dinner and if there was any left over they would have it for playlunch.

The next day they would wait and wait for the recess bell to ring. They would look at their watches and bite their nails.

RING RING RING

They rushed to their bags and got out their chocolate cake, went to the furtherest corner of the school yard, made sure no one was looking, peeled back the foil and there it was . . . .

THE CHOCOLATE CAKE . . .

The thick crackly chocolate icing,
Light fluffy cream,
Delicious and sticky raspberry jam and
The light soft sponge . . .

Next weekend was Tiffany's and Melissa's birthday. They wanted to spend their birthday together . . .

Kym, Olivia and Becky

Shape stories

After being shown some shape poetry a grade 2 child wrote this story:

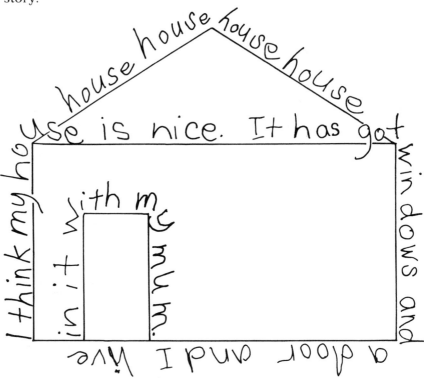

The connections between reading and writing are obvious throughout the above examples. Thorough immersion in various print models provides children with meaningful reading experiences which assist their writing tasks. During the process of proof-reading and editing, children are also engaged in reading.

Strategies and activities which integrate reading and writing are included below. They provide a range of styles for written presentation where children will be required to decide on the form most appropriate for their piece.

Reader's Theatre

Reader's Theatre is a popular strategy for having children write stories to be performed to an audience. This is the group reading of a story, read in parts by individuals, pairs or small groups of children who usually 'own' the story, that is, they have written an original piece or have worked on a previously known and favoured story. This strategy focuses on children reading the scripts to an audience rather than memorising chunks of text which often becomes tedious or threatening.

Having the support of the text during the performance gives readers of all abilities more control over their performance potential and ultimately their confidence as readers. This strategy has proved very successful with students across all ability levels including ESL and gifted children. Included below are some favourite examples.

A FAIRY TALE OR TWO

1, 2, 3   Once upon a time, in the woods, lived the three pigs.
1   Goldilocks was their next-door neighbour.
1, 2, 3   'Neighbours, everybody needs good neighbours.' (*to the tune of the TV show 'Neighbours'*)
2   Now these characters were living happily, until a wolf moved into the neighbourhood.
1, 2, 3   AND WHAT A HOOD HE WAS.
3   At night time, he would knock on their windows and scare them by pulling mean and ugly faces.
1, 2   This mean old wolf loved playing with matches and one day he accidentally burnt the pigs' house down.
1, 2, 3   SO THEY ALL WENT TO LIVE WITH GOLDILOCKS.
1   But not the wolf.
1, 2, 3   NO WAY!!!!!!!!

3   Goldilocks, however, just LOVED bacon. When the three
         pigs found this out, they took off to save THEIR bacon.
1, 2, 3 They went deep into the woods to live.
2   Meanwhile, the wolf decided to camp in these woods. He
         went to cook a roast dinner.
1, 2   When he looked in his bag there was no food.
2   That's when he smelt the pigs and said,
1, 2, 3 FE, FI, FO, FUM, I SMELL PIGS
         YUM, YUM, YUM, YUM.
3   So, he picked up his rifle and started hunting. Then he said,
1, 2, 3 'OOPPS, I FORGOT MY SALT AND PEPPER AND MY KNIFE
         AND FORK.'
1   While the wolf went to get his things, the three pigs saw
         him.
2, 3   They rang up Goldilocks. She pulled out two guns from her
         knickers and raced out to blow the wolf's tail off.
3   The wolf ran off without his tail between his legs.
1, 2, 3 And the three little pigs were safe.

                              ZEE END

                                        Marcus, Chris and Paul

KOALA LOU

1	Koala Lou was a nice and cuddly koala.
2 & 3	All the animals loved her.
4	Her mother loved her the most. She always said, 'KOALA LOU, I DO LOVE YOU.'
5 & 6	And she always smiled when she saw Koala Lou.
4	Koala Lou always went down the old track to find food for her and her sweet mother.
5	Her mother waved her hand and said, 'KOALA LOU, I *DO* LOVE YOU.'
3	This made Koala Lou very happy.
6	But her mother had a lot more babies to look after, and so she didn't say, 'KOALA LOU, I *DO* LOVE YOU' very much.
2 & 3 & 4	So Koala Lou thought and thought of how she could make her mother proud of her. She decided to enter the *Bush Olympics*.
1	Koala Lou exercised every day and put on her proper Olympic clothes.
All	She really wanted to win.
5	The day of the *Bush Olympics* came and Koala Lou entered the tree-climbing race.
3	Koala Klaws entered the tree-climbing race too.
2 & 4	Then the climbing race began. Koala Klaws went first. She was slow and Koala Lou beat her.
3	This made Koala Lou very happy and she went to find her mother, and her mother said,
All	'KOALA LOU, I *DO* LOVE YOU, BUT I WOULD STILL LOVE YOU EVEN IF YOU CAME LAST.'
4	They hugged each other and gave each other a kiss.
All	They lived happily ever after.

Natasha

CINDERELLA AND THE TWO DWARFS

SCENE 1

SONG 1
Cinderella and the two dwarfs,
Der, Der, Der, Der, Der, Der,
Cinderella and the two dwarfs,
Der, Der, Der, Der, Der, Der,
Cinderella and the two dwarfs,
That's the name of our story.
(CLAP) Der, Der, Der, Der, Der.

Dwarfs come on crying.

1	We've lost our job and
1 & 2	We're unemployed.
2	The machinery has taken over.
3	Don't worry, we've plenty of jobs at my place like
1	Cleaning the floor.
2	Washing the dishes.
3	Ironing the clothes.
4	Polishing the shoes
ALL	and
5	Making the beds.
2	Yeah, well
1	come along.
5	So the dwarfs came along with Cinderella to her place when suddenly
ALL	A prince walked in.
4	There will be a disco at my joint at 7.30.
3	Oh, drat, I won't get to see 'Neighbours'. It's
5	the wedding of
4	Scott
1	and
2	Charlene . . .

SCENE 2

5 At
3 the disco
4 there were
2 flashing lights
1 and loud music.

SONG 2
Cinderella dressed in yella,
Went to the disco to meet a fella.

4 Wanna dance baby?
3 Yeah, I'll dance with you right now.
5 They danced all night until she looked at her watch
ALL And it wasn't there.
1 & 2 So she asked the prince what the time was.
4 Precisely 12.01.
3 Oh no, Mum will kill me if I don't get home.
ALL Right away in my silver-lined Porsche.
5 When she
4 got home
2 her mother
1 killed her
ALL and she lived deadfully ever after.

SONG 3
Cinders is dead and the dwarfs are free.
Der, Der, Der, Der, Der,
Cinders is dead and the dwarfs are free,
Der, Der, Der, Der, Der,
Cinders is dead and the dwarfs are free,
That's the end of our stor-or-ie.
(*CLAP*) Der, Der, Der, Der, Der, Der.

Anna, Carolyn, Melissa, Michelle and Janelle

Literary events

After the reading or telling of a story, children can elect to be involved with any of the following activities:

- caption competition
- town criers and broadsheets
- questionnaires
- jam sessions
- poetry parties
- collage poetry.

Caption competition

After *Willy the Wimp* by Anthony Browne[4] was read to a grade 2 class, a large sheet of paper was hung near the door. It asked, 'Is Willy really a wimp?'. The children were encouraged to write their opinions on the sheet. The following ideas were recorded on a blackboard:

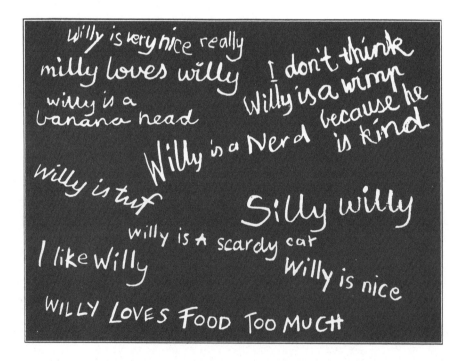

The class was so excited about their ideas that they decided to run a competition and vote for the best caption. To promote the competition the poster was displayed in the school library where Anthony Browne was the author for the month. Other classes were invited to vote for their favourite caption. The winner was 'Willy is a banana head'.

All this attention to the story led to much discussion and the class was then invited to tell its own stories about Willy. The children were brimming over with original ideas, such as the following:

Willy was a wimpy gorilla. He was short and he had pimples. One day a princess gorilla called Milly rescued him from the bad gang of gorillas. She said 'Oh Willy, I love you even if you've got pimples.' And Willy said 'I love you too.' They got married and went to live in Africa. The End.

Most of the *Willy* stories were sensitive to Willy's predicament which indicated the extent to which the children had internalised the author's meaning. What they had done with their own stories was to interpret Browne's version, making new meanings which were sympathetic to the original.

Town criers and broadsheets

The use of broadsheets and town criers is associated with the era prior to and immediately following the introduction of the printing press. Newspapers were scarce or not available and so worthy news items were published on broadsheets and the contents were called out by the town crier.

After a story experience, children are invited to rewrite an aspect of the original as an interesting news item. The following broadsheet was completed after a group of grade 6 children had read *Mrs Frisby and the Rats of NIMH*.[5]

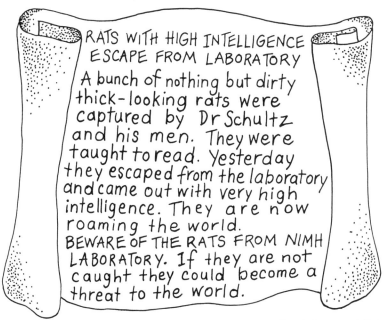

RATS WITH HIGH INTELLIGENCE ESCAPE FROM LABORATORY

A bunch of nothing but dirty thick-looking rats were captured by Dr Schultz and his men. They were taught to read. Yesterday they escaped from the laboratory and came out with very high intelligence. They are now roaming the world.
BEWARE OF THE RATS FROM NIMH LABORATORY. If they are not caught they could become a threat to the world.

Danielle and Michelle

The article was written up on large sheets of paper and made into a sandwich board. One child wore the broadsheet while his partner walked with him around the playground ringing a bell and calling out the text. You can imagine the excitement this would cause when a whole class or school becomes involved and the playground reverberates with town criers making proclamations from the sheets of text. A great treat for Bookweek!

There are various ways of displaying the broadsheets. Some could hang from classroom windows with the crier standing below to attract an audience. They could also be displayed along corridors or on notice boards.

Questionnaires

These are popular as a follow-up to a story. Classes who have a favourite author can devise a set of questions about the stories and the author. If the class is working in small groups, then one group can be responsible for drawing up the questionnaire. This could be distributed among the other class members or to other classes or schools who have also read the same author. Questionnaires based on the stories of Paul Jennings, Robin Klein and Gillian Rubinstein would be sure to receive successful feedback from a range of classes and schools. The teacher should encourage inferential or speculative questions rather than comprehension types. From the book *Unreal*[6] the following questions could be issued.

QUESTIONNAIRE

► Can you think of another setting which might be just as good for the story 'Without a Shirt?'
► Describe the inside of the lighthouse as Anton first walked up the spiral stairs to the top.
► Think of three things which Brian might do immediately after he had buried the bones.
► Stan and Anton protested against having the lighthouse pulled down. Can you think of any protests by people recently who try to support something they believe in?
► If you were looking for a salesperson to sell products for your business, would you employ Giffen? Why? Why not?
► Out of the eight stories in *Unreal*, which character did you like the most? Why? Why not?
  Who was the biggest bully? Why?
  Do you think any of the characters were similar? Explain.
  Could they be best friends?
► How popular do you think the hair removing cream would be?
  Who might use it and why?
► Which ghost story in this book is the best? Say why.

Jam sessions

In a jam session on traditional folk- and fairy-tales, some grade 5 and 6 boys made up the following rap songs.

THE WOODCUTTER'S STORY

Walking in the woods one Friday,
I saw Little Red Riding Hood coming my way.

She had a basket, it was small,
It reminded me of the one I saw in the mall.

I said 'Hi' and she said 'Hi',
Then she walked right past me and said 'Bye bye'.

I followed her back to an old wooden shack,
I saw an old hag sitting out the back.

I crept round behind the chair,
But the wolf had already beaten me there.

The wolf was furry and was grey,
It reminded me of the one I saw yesterday.

He made a lunge at the old hag,
But Little Red Riding Hood said, 'You're bad.'

The woodcutter threatened the wolf with an axe,
But the wolf decided he'd better make tracks.

Out that door he went with great speed,
But all he could think of was a good feed.

So that wolf came back
To that old wooden shack
Then he walked in the door
And slipped on the wet floor.

Little Red Riding Hood seized the chance
She broke his neck and did a dance.

Brad, Tony and Troy

THE THREE LITTLE PIGS

Well here's the story of the Three Little Pigs
A house made of straw and a house made of twigs.
The other little pig his brain will tick,
Cause he made his house right out of bricks.
Two little pigs for they got eaten, but the
other little pig is undefeated.
Now our little story it has to end, cause
We're got a real cool play to tend . . . .

Clinton

Poetry parties

We should encourage children to read and recite poems in many different and entertaining ways. This engagement with the text gives them greater control over the words and extends their confidence in reading aloud. To make the sessions more entertaining children could perform the pieces in the following ways:
- antiphonal recitals (sung or chanted alternately in pairs or groups)
- solos

- pairs
- using different emotional states
- in appropriate roles, for example as a stern old man, as a snobbish princess, as football supporters
- chanting in groups varying from loud rap and jazz styles to whispers and echoes in monotone styles.

The performance takes on a party atmosphere when: balloons and streamers are used to decorate the stage or classroom; background music accompanies certain pieces to add mood; the above performance styles are choreographed to provide a continuous medley of poetry, song, riddles and chants.

Collage poetry

When we think of collage we recall our attempts at artwork which relied on joining bits and pieces of paper cut-outs and other materials to create individual pieces. You can do the same with poetry. Collect titles of songs, chants from rhymes and jingles, glimpses of graffiti, book titles and string them together to create new and interesting pieces. Max Fatchen has created a collage poem entitled 'Summer Mail' from bits and pieces of letters in his book *A Paddock of Poems*.[7] An example of collage poetry is 'The Piggy Poem'.

THE PIGGY POEM

PIGS IS PIGS BOSS!

This little pig went to market,
This little pig stayed home.

*Meanwhile, back at the ranch
the three little pigs were
plotting against their enemy—
The Big Bad Wolf.*

Pork Pies
Pork Pies
Eat Them With Flies
Pork Pies

This little pig had McDonald's for dinner,
This little pig had none.

*They decided to build three
different types of houses to
confuse Old Wolf.*

PIGS FOR SALE!

And this little pig said,
'Rad Man, he won't catch you now'.

EPILOGUE
Jingle bells, old wolf smells
The three pigs got away
Oh what fun to see him boil
In a pot of bubbling oil, oh!

McBacon, McBacon, McBacon,
Three pigs ran off to the station,
They made it in time
To the other side of the line.

Q What did the piggy bank say when it fell off the table?
A I'm broke.

Children find this a challenging and exciting activity when they brainstorm ideas from known titles; display them and then allow groups to work on bringing the words and phrases together to form collage poetry.

Other activities that children could become involved in after a story-telling session include:
- song sheets
- poetry parade
- promotion posters
- graffiti wall
- proverbs.

Summary

Using the wealth of children's literature that is available to stimulate their imaginations, we not only provide them with the material to create their own worthy samples, we demonstrate to them the conventions of our language, both spoken and written. In the activities mentioned in this chapter, children have the opportunity to practise and use language at the literal level and so internalise the features and functions of text. At the same time they are creating, entertaining and playing with the ideas and rhythms of our most important asset—our ability to create and communicate by using language.

CHAPTER 9

Story across the curriculum

❝ Story-telling planned and carried out to fit conditions will help to solve many of the problems that confront educators to-day. Besides developing the emotional nature and giving moral and religious instruction, it will intensify the interest in history, geography, nature-study, manual training, and domestic science, awaken an appreciation of literature, art and music, enrich the children's powers of discrimination, teach him to distinguish between the cheap and ephemeral and the great and lasting.[1] ❞

....

Historical perspective

Katherine Dunlap Cather realised the power of story in education when she wrote her text *Educating by Story-telling* which was published in 1919. Prior to this date she had been advocating and practising the teaching of children using the medium of story. Her ideas are impressive because they developed in a period when traditional methods of education were entrenched. The traditional method espoused the model of teaching from the known and concrete to the unknown and abstract. This model has remained the most popular theory for learning along with the Piagetian view of relative logical thinking.

Cather's philosophy for teaching through story centred on the power of emotional response in the act of learning. She believed that if children are emotionally moved by a piece of knowledge or information, then they will have a much greater chance of understanding and therefore remembering the content or concepts than if they receive this information via traditional channels.

Cather rightly believed that we more often recall the tales and tunes heard in our early years than we do the content of classroom learning. Her text yields various stories categorised under curriculum headings which reveal different concepts and ideas.

To study geography, now included in general studies, Cather included a series of stories from other regions that conveyed ideas and understandings about different cultures and peoples. If, for instance, a class was looking at the customs and beliefs of American

Indians you could tell the Iroquois legend 'The God of the Thundering Water'[2] to familiarise children with the Indian marriage custom and to introduce the physical characteristics of North American landmarks such as Niagara Falls. These ideas may be researched as part of a larger unit on America.

If children are to learn successfully, they need to exercise their imagination. If learning a series of dates in chronological order for history, they need not focus on dull time-lines as memory aids. Rather, these moments in history can be woven around stories from the past. The outcome will be an arousal of imaginative interest which will result in a higher level of understanding.

Nature lends itself to story because many scientific facts echo plot structure. For example, the life-cycle of a butterfly is a wonderful story with a definite beginning, middle and end where the caterpillar changes via a cocoon into a butterfly. Eric Carle has captured this feat of nature in his popular story *The Very Hungry Caterpillar* where the character eats himself through the seven days of the week to emerge as a butterfly after spending three weeks in his cocoon.[3] This story has endless possibilities across the curriculum, including maths concepts of time, days of the week and periods longer than a week; health issues involving junk food versus health food; art concepts in distinguishing the primary colours used in the illustrations.

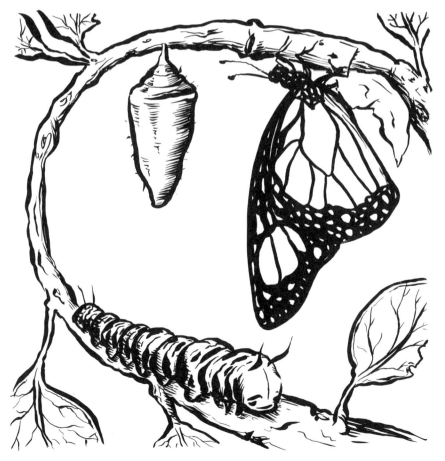

Making meaning through inferences

Previous chapters have referred to the power of inference as a creative learning tool. Not only can children infer meaning about characters and setting or the outcome of a story, but they can infer knowledge, ideas and concepts which arise from the context of a story.

Edie Garvie clearly demonstrates how this can happen in her text *Story as Vehicle*, which looks at teaching English as a second language to children.[4] She lists five stages which she thinks children go through in order to develop concepts:

- *Identification*:   labelling, identifying objects
- *Qualification*:   describing attributes, for example, size, shape
- *Relation*:   comparison of above known concepts noting similarities and differences
- *Classification*:   sorting into categories
- *Manipulation*:   using concepts to hypothesise, especially cause and effect, using imagination to fantasise.

Pamela Allen's story *Who Sank The Boat?*[5] can be used to show how easily children can infer meaning about a whole range of concepts:

- identification: children can label and name the animals who appear in the story
- qualification: each character is portrayed with distinctive physical characteristics which the children can identify
- relation: the distinctive qualities of each character reveal comparisons which become obvious to the children who see them within the context of the story
- classification: the animals are presented in an ordinal pattern which reveals to children the hierarchy of size
- manipulation: when faced with the central question of the plot, 'Who sank the boat?', children are motivated to hypothesise which animal will cause the boat to tip and sink. Much imaginative discussion follows.

Imagination and learning

In his text *Teaching as Storytelling*, Kieran Egan also recognises the value of story in education and takes up the challenge of similar ideas.[6] He stresses the importance of the link between memory, emotion and imagination, arguing that story is a means of organising content, thus making it memorable. If the story is worthy then the children will be emotionally committed to it.

This response is what Egan sees as making learning meaningful. 'To present knowledge cut off from human emotions and intentions is to reduce its affective meaning.'[7] If children are affected by the story-line, their engagement will ensure a pathway for access to the content.

The notion that children learn from the concrete and known to the abstract and unknown is refuted by Egan who says that, due to the natural predisposition of the young to understand the concepts in story, for example, good, evil, jealousy, etc., they are better able to accept and comprehend such ideas within the framework of story structure which is a known quantity: '. . . new content can be structured on 'known' abstract categories, or . . . it [can] be a mediation between 'known' binary opposites.'[8]

Rather than beginning a unit or lesson with a statement of objectives, Egan advocates that teachers set up binary opposites within which the content will be effectively organised; according to Egan children will comprehend the concepts and ideas because they are presented in the familiar story format. And so the binary opposites become the focus of the unit.

The following unit is based on Egan's ideas. All units are planned and taught around his five-stage model.[9]

Story form model

The Story Form Model

1 Identifying importance
- What is most important about the topic?
- Why should it matter to children?
- What is affectively engaging about it?

2 Finding binary opposites
- What powerful binary opposites best catch the importance of the topic?

3 Organising content into story form
- What content most dramatically embodies the binary opposites, in order to provide access to the topic?
- What content best articulates the topic into a developing story form?

4 Conclusion
- What is the best way of resolving the dramatic conflict inherent in the binary opposites?
- What degree of mediation of those opposites is it appropriate to seek?

5 Evaluation
- How can one know whether the topic has been understood, its importance grasped, and the content learned?

Three grade 6 teachers from Eltham College in Victoria devised a term's work based on Egan's model, integrating all areas of the curriculum. The topic was 'The environment—future worlds' and was tackled in the following way.

Topic: The Environment— Future Worlds

1 Identifying importance

Q What is most important about the topic?
A That we look from the past to the present and then to the future well-being of our world.

Q Why should it matter to children?
A The children realise they have a responsibility in helping the world to survive in the future.

As an introduction to the unit, the following story was told and the children were given an acorn seed to nurture:

> I am on a journey: rather a long and involved one that will take me many places and teach me many things. You, too, are coming on that journey and I hope that you will gain much from it.
>
> There will be conflict along the way and you will need to make decisions: not all of them easy. Not everything will be as you would like it.
>
> But, always, in the face of despair, there will be hope. And it is that hope that will keep us all going.
>
> To help keep that hope strong, I wish to give you something to cling to: an acorn seed—it may not seem to be much, but it signifies a great deal and I would like you to think carefully about its significance. Take care of it—it is what hope is built on.[10]

Q What is affectively engaging about it?

A The children chose a local patch of land which had become an environmental nightmare and it was obvious that they felt strongly about reclaiming it.

2 Finding binary opposites

Q What powerful binary opposites best catch the importance of the topic?

A The three teachers brainstormed ideas for the binary opposites:

survival	destruction
adventure	frustration
hope	desperation
excitement	desolation
joy	no-point
fulfilment	useless
harmony	devastation
building	negativeness
to give	negligence
faith	anger
laughter	
confidence	
sense of peace	
worthwhile	
hopeful	

These extensive lists were then narrowed down to three pairs of opposites:

peace—war
harmony—imbalance
confidence—desperation

Finally they focused on the opposites of HOPE and DESPAIR. To demonstrate these opposites the picture-book *The Man Who Planted Trees*[11] was used. This was read in stages throughout the unit so the children could gain a sense of change from DESPAIR to HOPE as this wonderful story unfolded. To further impress the idea of the binary opposites on the children, a video of the text was also played in stages.[12]

3 Organising content into story form

Q What content most dramatically embodies the binary opposites, in order to provide access to the topic?

A The term's curriculum was planned to encompass the binary opposites as set out in detail in appendix 1 (pp. 110–13).

Q What content best articulates the topic into a developing story form?

A The local patch of land known as 'Dilly's Gate' became the focus for change from DESPAIR to HOPE. Children were taken to the site with the view to drawing comparisons between the developing story in Giono's text and the future possibilities for reclaiming this desolate tract. All content across the curriculum was linked via related activities to 'Dilly's Gate'.

4 Conclusion

Q What is the best way of resolving the dramatic conflict inherent in the binary opposites?

A By bringing the unit to a natural conclusion which is satisfactory for the participants. This follows the pattern of story-orientation, complication, resolution.

Q What degree of mediation of those opposites is it appropriate to seek?

A We seek to have the children understand that there will always be times when despair will exist, but that it is the hope for the future, born out of that despair, which will make the future possible. Certainly, viewing the video 'The Man Who Planted Trees' in its entirety, as the culmination of the unit, will show the relationship between the binary opposites and how despair can lead to hope.

5 Evaluation

Q How can one know whether the topic has been understood, its importance grasped, and the content learned?

A The following stories and poems (pp. 100–6) reveal the degree to which the children grasped the binary opposites and the story of our changing environment.

Other methods used to evaluate the children's understanding of the topic included:
- observation
- discussion
- anecdotal records
- samples of children's work
- the degree of commitment and involvement in the tasks
- review sheets, for example maths.

POSSUM

The possum sat silently on a tree branch. Nearly all the birds had left the tree because people kept coming into the small forest and the birds had sensed danger. They found new places to live, but possum thought he was tough enough to handle them, besides, he had nowhere to go.

Possum woke up to hear the sound of a motor starting up. He didn't think it was anything but the stupid people's car which stank out the joint, until the tree started to vibrate so much that he was nearly thrown out of the tree. He now sat up and looked down. THEY WERE CUTTING DOWN HIS TREE!!!

The possum looked around for a tree to jump onto but all the trees around had been cut down. He suddenly felt the tree tip backwards, slowly at first, then faster and faster. All he could do was hold on and wait. Fear shot through him like a lightning bolt. He dared not move but he couldn't stay where he was! TOO LATE!!!!!!

CRASH!!!!!!! Possum just sat there. That was the only thing he could do. He felt as though every bone in his body had been broken.

Possum was aching all over. He just lay there seeing which part of his body he could move. He could move his head, back and one arm. Possum heard someone shout, 'Look at this!', but he didn't take much notice until soft warm hands closed around him. He really thought he was a 'gonner' now.

But to his amazement, the face was a lady's and it was soft and gentle. She placed him in a blanket after a lot of fuss and bother, put him in a car and drove away. The possum was taken to the vet, definitely against his will. But he felt much better for it, they put his leg and arm in splints and he was taken to the lady's house. The lady petted and fussed over him a great deal more than she should have and about the only thing she said was, 'You're so cute aren't you', and she said that every two seconds.

The 6 weeks it took for his leg to heal passed slowly for the possum and although the lady was very nice, he missed home. He kept forgetting his home was no more.

At the end of 6 weeks the lady freed him in a flood of tears. She let him go in a massive forest. He couldn't believe his eyes; it was so, so, so huge. He would miss the lady and his old home very much, but for now he had to explore!

Katherine

SHYLY

'Who are you?' Shyly asked as a flash of light entered her room from the roof and standing there was a beautiful girl with snow white skin, black hair and big brown eyes. The girl said that her name was Annie and she had come from Gumsville, a world of nature. Shyly didn't believe her but told Annie to say more about herself and why she had come to her at 2:00 in the morning. Annie explained to Shyly about her world and how she lived without electricity, chemicals or plastics etc. and why she had come to Shyly. Annie said that her queen, Mother Nature, had sent 50 boys and girls to go to other boys and girls on earth and warn them about skin cancer, pollution, greenhouse effect and many other environmental issues. Shyly started to believe Annie and questioned her over and over again. As Annie was talking Shyly noticed that Annie was wearing a beautiful white dress, so when Annie had finished talking Shyly asked her how she had made her dress. She said it was from silk produced by Silk Worms. Shyly was amazed and fascinated by this. Annie kept talking but Shyly must have fallen asleep because the last thing she remembered was Annie telling her to CARE FOR THE EARTH!!

At breakfast the next morning, Shyly told her mother about Annie and how she had come during the night. She also told her how she shouldn't use CFCs, not to use her car so much and to recycle waste products. Shyly's mother's eyes turned from wide, interested, kind eyes to dark, narrow and mean eyes.

'Nonsense!', she cried, 'you're making it up and you know it!'

'I'm not,' Shyly tried to say, but her mother just told her to eat her cornflakes and if she wasn't going to speak the truth, not to speak at all.

As she ate her breakfast her father left to go to his job as a logger. She thought about what Annie had said to her about how we need trees to give us oxygen to make us breathe. Shyly told him about what he was doing to the earth by cutting them down and if he didn't stop doing it the earth would heat up. Her father only said that it was his job and it was because of this that she had a roof over her head and she had no right telling him what and what not to do!

Shyly kept telling her parents about the earth's problem, but the more she talked about it, the more annoyed her parents became. They continued using CFCs and eating fast food from foam packaging. Every night Annie visited Shyly and told her more about the environment.

After about 1 year, in the year 2098, the earth's climate had increased by 17 degrees C and the average temperature was about 43 degrees C. Shyly did all she could to try and tell people to preserve the earth but no one listened. Most people wore masks around and 70% of people had skin cancer. About 96% of trees had gone. All the grass had turned brown and there was a drought. The ground was red and burned your feet to walk on it. It hadn't rained for 11 months and people were committing suicide.

Finally, the day came. The morning was hot and still and by 10:00 a.m. it was 54 C. The temperature kept rising and by 3:00 it was 87 C. Things were melting and people were dissolving. The sun beat down with furious force. Shyly lay on the ground with her cat covered completely by clothes. Fortunately, Annie arrived. She grabbed Shyly and her cat and took them with her back to Gumsville. When they had almost reached the planet, Gumsville, they saw earth blow up in a mass of red flames. It was blown into a million pieces of glowing red flames. Shyly shut her eyes to hold back her tears.

When she opened her eyes again she found she was in a cool, green, fresh land.

'Is this Gumsville?' Shyly asked.

'Yes, this is Gumsville.'

'I can't believe this is true', Shyly thought. As she walked around she noticed that there were no shops, roads, houses or cars.

As Shyly made friends with people there, she thought how they deserved such a fine land. How she wished her old friends or family were here to show them what kind of land she belonged in and fought for. But it didn't matter. She was in peace now. The birds flew over and an elephant wandered past. And as she looked up in the sky she saw a fire ball coming towards her. She jumped as it landed and saw a spray can on it. She grabbed it and buried it, hoping that the people of Gumsville would not make the same mistake as she had.

Tory

Snow is white, soft on the tip of the mountains,
rich ice-cream sitting on a silver spoon,
A small soft cygnet and the light
of the moon.
White is pure, fresh and clean, petals
of a daisy, crisp white sheet,
Waves that are crashing on the
rocks, frost on a foggy morning

Black is the colour of eerie dark alleyways,
The colour of death, the cape of a ghoul.
Black is the colour of a dead man's coffin,
The colour a soul would wear to a funeral.
Black is the colour of a graveyard at night,
The feeling of emptiness-yet life among death.
Black is the colour of a witch's black cat,
A mysterious colour- that colour of Black.

YOUNG
free, innocent
caring, loving, playing
children, kittens, Grandma, Grandpa,
suffering, dying, worrying
miserable, lonely,
OLD

RICH
glamorous, wealthy,
glittering, stunning, spending,
filmstar, millionaire, tramp, beggar,
pleading, wanting, grieving,
homeless, hungry
POOR

White is a daisy pretty and neat,
White is the snow on a very fine peak,
White is a searing hot heat,
White are the waves with their tiny white tips,
White is fresh milk ready to drink,
White is the feeling when ready to think.
White is a batch of hanging clouds,
White is a field of cotton bold,
White is crisp,
White is clean,
White is a sheet with its edging so seen,
White is peaceful, white is neat, white is a
simple but nice colour don't you think?

Purple is the taste of fresh grapejuice,
The taste of grape-flavoured bubble-gum,
Purple is the beginning of light after dark.
Purple is the colour of a light bulb before
it blows.
Purple is the colour of smooth, silky velvet
or a violet's petals scattered on the ground.
Purple is the happiness of a new friend.
Purple is the sadness of a lost, best friend.

SAD
DEPRESSED, MISERABLE,
CRYING, SCREAMING, WANTING,
DEATH, HURT, BIRTH, LIFE
PLAYING, CELEBRATING, ENJOYING
CHEERY, BRIGHT
HAPPY

COLD

Snow, White

Freezing, Snowing, Chilling

Frozen, Icy, Burn, Sear

Burning, Boiling, Sizzling

Sun, Fire

HOT

. . . .

Summary

We have looked at three twentieth century educators—Cather, Garvie and Egan—who have espoused effective learning via story and story-telling. Each approach is individual in design but they are united in their belief in the power of the story form to communicate ideas and knowledge. All three educators believe that it is the emotional response to knowledge that makes learning meaningful, and that if children can draw on their natural powers of imagination in response to content which has affected them, then effective learning will indeed have taken place.

Notes

Chapter 1

1 Aidan Chambers, 'The Child's Changing Story' in *Signal*, No. 40, 1983, p. 36.
2 June Factor, *Unreal, Banana Peel!*, Oxford University Press, Melbourne, 1986, p. 48.
3 Anon., 'Miss Mary Mack' in *Yickity-yackity yickity-yak* (comp. David Drew & Denise Ryan), Oxford University Press, Melbourne, 1990, p. 12.

Chapter 2

1 Norma Livo & Sandra Rietz, *Storytelling: Process and Product*, Libraries Unlimited Inc., Colorado, 1986, p. 2.

Chapter 3

1 Patricia Scott, 'The Ways of Storytelling' in *Magpies*, Vol. 1, No. 1., March 1986, p. 5.
2 Anne Commire (ed.), *Something About the Author, Vol. 48*, Gale Research Inc., London, 1986, p. 196.
3 Michael Rosen, *Quick, Let's Get Out of Here*, Penguin Books Ltd, London, 1985, p. 14.

Chapter 4

1 Bob Barton & David Booth, *Stories in the Classroom*, Heinemann, Portsmouth (NH), 1990, p. 9.
2 Jiri Trnka (illust.), *Fairy Tales of Hans Christian Andersen*, Paul Hamlyn, London, 1959.
3 Maurice Sendak, *Where the Wild Things Are*, Penguin, Harmondsworth, in association with The Bodley Head, 1970.
4 In Morris Lurie, *Night Night*, Oxford University Press, Melbourne, 1987.

Chapter 5

1 Quoted in Woutrina Bone, *Children's Stories and How to Tell Them*, Harcourt, Brace & Co., Detroit, 1975, p. 7.
2 Michael Rosen, *Hairy Tales and Nursery Crimes*, Collins, London, 1987.
3 Rosen, *Hairy Tales and Nursery Crimes*, p. 76.
4 Rosen, *Hairy Tales and Nursery Crimes*, p. 28.
5 Paul Galdone, *The Little Red Hen*, Scholastic, New York, 1973.
6 Cecilia Egan, *Little Red Riding Hood*, Egan Publishing Pty Ltd, Bentleigh (Vic.), 1988.
7 Maurice Sendak, *Where the Wild Things Are*, Penguin, Harmondsworth, in association with The Bodley Head, 1970.
8 Camilla Gryski, *Cat's Cradle and Other String Stories*, Angus & Robertson, North Ryde (NSW), 1985.
9 Anne Pellowski, *The Story Vine*, Collier Books, New York, 1984.
10 Henry Lawson, 'The Ballad of the Drover' in *Victorian Readers, Fifth Book*, Ministry of Education, Melbourne, 1986.
11 Ruth Atkinson *et al.*, *Down Amongst Gum Leaves*, Dominie, Brookvale (NSW), 1990.
12 Jean Stangl, *Paper Stories*, David S. Lake Publishers, Belmont (CA), 1987.
13 Bill Martin Jr & John Archambault, *The Ghost-Eye Tree*, Orchard Books, London, 1986.
14 Morris Lurie, 'The Talking Bow Tie' in *Night Night*, Oxford University Press, Melbourne, 1987.

Chapter 6

1 Lucy McCormick Calkins, *The Art of Teaching Writing*, Heinemann, Portsmouth (NH), 1986, p. 124.
2 Jacob & Wilhelm Grimm, 'Mother Snowbed' in *Selected Tales*, Penguin Books Ltd, Ringwood (Vic.), 1982.
3 Joy Cowley, *Tom's Trousers*, Murdoch Books, North Ryde (NSW).

Chapter 7

1 Judith Wells Lindfors, *Children's Language and Learning* (2nd edn), Prentice-Hall Inc., Englewood Cliffs (NJ), 1987, p. 357.

Chapter 8

1 K. Goodman & Y. Goodman, 'Learning to read is natural' in *Theory and Practice of Early Reading, Vol. 1* (eds L. Rennick & P. A. Weaver), Laurence Erlbaum Associates, Hillsdale (NJ), 1979, p. 150.
2 Hazel Brown & Brian Cambourne, *Read and Retell*, Methuen, North Ryde (NSW), 1987, p. 15.
3 Morris Lurie, 'The Talking Bow Tie' in *Night Night*, Oxford University Press, Melbourne, 1987.
4 Anthony Browne, *Willy the Wimp*, Methuen, London, 1986.
5 Robert O'Brien, *Mrs Frisby and the Rats of NIMH*, Puffin Books, London, 1975.
6 Paul Jennings, *Unreal*, Penguin Books Ltd, Ringwood (Vic.), 1985.
7 Max Fatchen, *A Paddock of Poems*, Omnibus/Puffin, Ringwood (Vic.), 1987.

Chapter 9

1 Katherine Dunlap Cather, *Educating By Story-telling*, George G. Harrap & Co. Ltd, London, 1919, pp. 33–4.
2 Cather, p. 204.
3 Eric Carle, *The Very Hungry Caterpillar*, Puffin Books, Ringwood (Vic.), 1974.
4 Edie Garvie, *Story As Vehicle: Teaching English to Young Children*, Multilingual Matters Ltd, Clevedon (PA), 1990, p. 54.
5 Pamela Allen, *Who Sank the Boat?*, Puffin Books, Ringwood (Vic.), 1982.
6 Kieran Egan, *Teaching As Storytelling*, Routledge, London, 1988.
7 K. Egan, p. 30.
8 K. Egan, p. 16.
9 K. Egan, p. 41.
10 Text created by Kathy Saville.
11 Jean Giono, *The Man Who Planted Trees*, Collins-Dove, Melbourne, 1989.
12 The video, together with the book, is available through Collins-Dove, Melbourne.

Integrated curriculum approach

The Man Who Planted Trees

....

Suggested activities

Language

Picture-book writing

The children are asked to write and illustrate books for the year 1's. The books are to have an environmental flavour, and carry the notions of despair and hope somewhere in the story. Illustrations could be created in conjunction with the art teacher, where the use of colour is significant, as it is in the story, *The Man Who Planted Trees*.

Novel study: *The Cay*

Although primarily a story about survival, the notions of hope and despair are very apparent throughout the story. Activities could include:

a writing character sketches of Timothy and/or Phillip, where their personal feelings of despair and hope are highlighted

b Phillip's mother writing to relatives in America relating the despair in the tragedy of his loss

c writing a newspaper article for a Curaçao Island paper, which focuses on the despair of a local resident's loss

d composing a prayer, which could have been said by Phillip, Phillip's father or mother, before, during or after the ordeal.

Poetry

a Using *Hailstones and Halibut Bones* and the colour changes in the story as a lead-in, the children are asked to write their own colour poems.

b Using the diamond (or diamente) pattern form, the children write diamond poems where pairs of opposites are used, for example despair/hope, love/hate, young/old, etc. (see examples on pp. 102–6).

c The children can bring their own favourite nature poems to the class, share them, write them up and a class anthology of favourite poems with a nature focus could result.

Mathematics

Area and perimeter

Children are given a variety of measuring implements, for example trundle wheels, measuring tapes, string, their feet, metre rulers, etc., to measure out and map the perimeter of a specified area.

Time

Time-lines of past important events can be created around the classroom and the concepts of BC, AD, and centuries can be explored.

Grids, scale and enlarging

Individual, paired and group activities can help children to enlarge pictures accurately. A large wall mural, with a nature and hope theme could be created.

Volume, displacement and graphing

Using the 'MCTP' pack (pp. 247–52), and *Mr Archimedes' Bath*, introduce volume, displacement and graphing. Practical measuring activities could evolve.

Social studies

Australia 2020

a Using the Gould League publication, *Australia 2020*, the children are asked to make decisions about future life-styles.

b Resulting futures can be discussed in relation to the hope and/or despair that their chosen future shows.

c Future stories are modified by making appropriate selections for a desired future in which hope is more apparent.

Science

Earthkeepers

A programme run by the Board of Works, in conjunction with the Institute of Earth Education, the programme involves the children spending 3 days at a local bush park, where stories and props are used to make the children aware of the hope and despair in our world today. The children's awareness is strengthened by the activities and the practical work which is completed back in the classroom. Similar activities can be undertaken, using the manual 'Conceptual Encounters', from which many of the *Earthkeepers* activities are drawn.

Seeds

Activities could include:

a classification of assorted seeds (use the story *The Seed* as an introductory stimulus)

b testing various conditions for those most suited to growth

c looking at the dispersal of seeds

d growing and nurturing seeds to maturation.

Regeneration

A particular area of the school (where feelings of despair in the children are clear) could be targeted for improvement, for example:

a clearing of rubbish

b planting of seedlings and trees

c making and placing of bird boxes to encourage bird-life back into the area.

Such activities provide a sense of ownership and help improve feelings of hope in our future.

Computer Studies

Space Station Nada

This is a BBC program, which uses logical thinking skills to help the children make decisions which result in either hope or despair in their character's life. Other computer programs could be used to highlight similar areas.

Health

Environmental Health

Suggestions for suitable activities can be found in the South Australian teaching guidelines, 'Health Education: Years 5–7, for example:

a in groups, write definitions for the natural environment, the man-made environment and the social environment and discuss

b make two puppets, one from a healthy environment (one full of hope) and the other from an unhealthy environment (one full of despair). Plan and act out a conversation (story) in which the puppets describe their environments to each other

c construct a collage from magazine pictures to show people responding to their environments.

Drama

Lost on a deserted island

Simulation activities could include:

a keeping and writing log entries in which the character expresses emotions of despair and hope

b looking at ways of using the natural environs in which one is lost so as to deal with the basics of survival, including water and food collection, clothing, and shelter, and dramatising these in small groups.

Art

See Language section for suggested suitable activities (pp. 110–11).

Music

The parameter of music can be explored as a compositional tool for the manipulation of sound until it sounds or feels like the binary opposites of hope and despair, for example:

a rhythm—despair: slow repetitions of patterns, never silent beats
        —hope: bouncy, snappy patterns, contrasts and variety
b expression—despair: muddy timbres, very slow changes in dynamics
        —hope: clear and contrasting timbres, exciting changes of dynamics, etc.

Library

Watching videos

View David Attenborough-type videos:

a so as to expose children to this type of documentary
b and use the videos to enable children to take notes from a visual medium.

Making videos

a After viewing several such videos, children could be asked to write and rehearse their own script for a three minute video which focuses on some of the most urgent of today's environmental issues, and where they can portray despair and hope prevalent in our world today.
b Each child is video-taped and the class views and discusses each three minute segment.

Bibliography

Allen, Pamela. *Mr. Archimedes' Bath*. Collins, Melbourne, 1985.

Cock, Peter, Farrow, Melanie & Crossley, David. *Australia 2020*. Gould League, Prahran, 1980.

Education Department of South Australia. *Health Education: Years 5–7 Teachers' Handbook*. Publications Branch, Adelaide, 1978.

Giono, Jean. *The Man Who Planted Trees*. Collins Dove, Blackburn, 1989.

Lovitt, Charles & Clarke, Doug. *Mathematics and Teaching Program. (M.C.T.P) Volumes 1 & 2*. Curriculum Development Centre, Canberra, 1988.

Nakazawa, Kazuko. *The Seed*. Hove, Wayland, 1978.

O'Neill, Mary. *Hailstones and Halibut Bones*. Tadworth, Surrey, 1962.

Primary Mathematics Project Team. *Mathematics Curriculum Guide: Measurement Guides*. Education Department of Victoria, Melbourne, 1981.

Taylor, Theodore. *The Cay*. Puffin, Ringwood, 1969.

vanMatre, Steve. *Conceptual Encounters*. The Institute for Earth Education, Illinois, 1987.

Bibliography

Allen, Pamela. *Who Sank The Boat?* Puffin, Ringwood (Vic.), 1982.

Atkinson, Ruth, Dalgliesh, Sharon & Mercer, Jeff. *Down Amongst Gum Leaves*. Dominie, Brookvale (NSW), 1990.

Barton, Bob & Booth, David. *Stories In The Classroom*. Heinemann, Portsmouth (NH), 1990.

Bone, Woutrina. *Children's Stories and How To Tell Them*. Harcourt, Brace & Co., Detroit, 1975.

Brown, Hazel & Cambourne, Brian. *Read and Retell*. Methuen, North Ryde (NSW), 1987.

Browne, Anthony. *Willy The Wimp*. Methuen, London, 1986.

Calkins, Lucy McCormick. *The Art of Teaching Writing*. Heinemann, Portsmouth (NH), 1986.

Carle, Eric. *The Very Hungry Caterpillar*. Puffin Books, Ringwood (Vic.), 1974.

Cather, Katherine Dunlap. *Educating By Story-telling*. George G. Harrap & Co. Ltd, London, 1919.

Chambers, Aidan. 'The Child's Changing Story' in *Signal*, No. 40, The Thimble Press, Stroud, Glos., Jan. 1983.

Commire, Anne (ed.). *Something About The Author*. Vol. 48, Gale Research Inc., London, 1987.

Cowley, Joy. *Tom's Trousers*. Murdoch Books, North Sydney, no date.

Drew, David & Ryan, Denise (comp.). *Yickity-yackity, yickity-yak*. Oxford University Press, Melbourne, 1990.

Egan, Cecilia. *Little Red Riding Hood*. Egan Publishing Pty Ltd, Bentleigh (Vic.), 1988.

Egan, Kieran. *Teaching As Storytelling*. Routledge, London, 1988.

Factor, June. *Far Out Brussel Sprout*. Oxford University Press, Melbourne, 1983.

Factor, June. *Unreal, Banana Peel!* Oxford University Press, Melbourne, 1990.

Fatchen, Max. *A Paddock of Poems*. Penguin, Ringwood (Vic.), 1987.

Galdone, Paul. *The Little Red Hen*. Scholastic, New York, 1973.

Garvie, Evie. *Story As Vehicle: Teaching English To Young Children*. Multilingual Matters Ltd, Clevedon (PA), 1990.

Giono, Jean. *The Man Who Planted Trees*. Collins-Dove, Melbourne, 1989.

Goodman, K. & Goodman, Y. 'Learning To Read Is Natural' in Rennick, Lauren & Weaver, P. A. (eds) *Theory & Practice of Early Reading, Vol. 1*. Laurence Erlbaum Associates, Hillsdale (NJ), 1979.

Grimm, Jacob & Wilhelm. *Selected Tales*. Penguin Books Ltd, Ringwood (Vic.). 1982.

Gryski, Camilla. *Cat's Cradle and Other Stories*. Angus & Robertson, North Ryde (NSW), 1985.

Jennings, Paul. *Unreal*. Penguin, Ringwood (Vic.), 1985.

Lawson, Henry. 'The Ballad of the Drover' in *Victorian Readers, Fifth Book*. Ministry of Education, Melbourne, 1986.

Lindfors, Judith Wells. *Children's Language and Learning* (2nd edn). Prentice-Hall Inc., Englewood Cliffs (NJ), 1987.

Livo, Norma & Rietz, Sandra. *Storytelling: Process and Product*. Libraries Unlimited Inc., Littleton (CO), 1986.

Lurie, Morris. *Night Night*. Oxford University Press, Melbourne, 1987.

Martin Jr, Bill & Archambault, John. *The Ghost-Eye Tree*. Orchard Books, London, 1986.

O'Brien, Robert. *Mrs Frisby And The Rats Of NIMH*. Penguin, London, 1975.

Pellowski, Anne. *The Story Vine*. Collier Books, New York, 1984.

Rosen, Michael. *Hairy Tales And Nursery Crimes*. Collins, London, 1987.

Rosen, Michael. *Quick, Let's Get Out Of Here*. Penguin, London, 1985.

Sendak, Maurice, *Where the Wild Things Are*. Penguin, Harmondsworth, in association with The Bodley Head, 1970.

Stangl, Jean. *Paper Stories*. David S. Lake Publishers, Belmont (CA), 1987.

Trnka, Jiri (illust.). *Fairy Tales of Hans Christian Andersen*. Hamlyn, London, 1959.

Further Resources

Barton, Bob. *Tell Me Another*. Pembroke Publishers, Markham, Ontario, 1986.

Chatfield, Heather & Lacey, Shirley. *Let's Enjoy Poetry*. Longman Cheshire, Melbourne, 1989.

Dunn, Sonja. *Butterscotch Dreams: Chants For Fun and Learning*. Pembroke Publishers, Markham, Ontario, 1987.

Factor, June. *Captain Cook Chased A Chook*. Penguin, Ringwood (Vic.), 1988.

Ferguson, Virginia & Durkin, Peter. *Rotten Apples: Top Stories To Read And Tell*. Thomas Nelson, Melbourne, 1989.

Graham, Carolyn. *Jazz Chant: Fairy Tales*. Oxford University Press, Melbourne, 1988.

Hill, Susan. *Raps & Rhymes*. Eleanor Curtain Publishing, South Yarra, 1990.

Jones, Terry. *Fairy Tales*. Puffin Books, Ringwood (Vic.), 1981.

Lee, Dennis. *Jelly Belly: Original Nursery Rhymes*. Macmillan, London, 1987.

Livo, Norma J. & Rietz, Sandra A. *Storytelling Activities*. Libraries Unlimited Inc., Littleton (CO), 1987.

Robinson, Moira. *Make My Toenails Twinkle: The Complete Resource Book For Sharing Poetry With Children*. Longman Cheshire, Melbourne, 1989.

Rosen, Betty. *And None Of It Was Nonsense*. Scholastic, Warwickshire, England, 1988.

Acknowledgements

I sincerely thank Libby Strain and John Wolf of Victoria College, Malvern, for use of their character-model activity. I am also grateful to Kathy Saville of Eltham College, and her colleagues Miranda Armstrong and Ann Connolly, for access to their teaching unit based on Kieran Egan's story form model. I cannot thank Diane Snowball enough for her enthusiasm and guidance which helped me to draw together my ideas. The photographic work by Simon Fox, Educational Media Services, Victoria College, and Keith Hulstaert is gratefully acknowledged. I extend special thanks to my husband Paul for his patience when the word-processor would not co-operate with me and for putting up with 'the back of my head' for all these months.

The author and publishers are grateful to copyright holders for permission to reproduce copyright material. Copyright holders and/or sources are as follows:

André Deutsch for 'Chocolate Cake' by Michael Rosen, from *Quick, Let's Get Out of Here!*; the Brothers Grimm, 'Mother Snowbed' from *Selected Tales*, published by Penguin Books Ltd; Routledge for the story form model by Kieran Egan, from *Teaching as Storytelling*.

Index